MINUTE
GUIDE TO
WinFax PRO

Joe Kraynak

alpha books

A Division of Prentice Hall Computer Publishing

201 West 103rd Street, Indianapolis, Indiana 46290 USA

To my kids, Nick and Ali, for making me laugh.

©**1994 by Alpha Books**

International Standard Book Number: 1-56761-406-X

Library of Congress Catalog Card Number: 93-73711

97 96 95 94   8 7 6 5 4 3 2

Interpretation of the printing code: the rightmost double-digit number is the year of the book's first printing; the rightmost single-digit number is the number of the book's printing. For example, a printing code of 94-1 shows that this copy of the book was printed during the first printing of the book in 1994.

Publisher: *Marie Butler-Knight*

Managing Editor: *Elizabeth Keaffaber*

Product Development Manager: *Faithe Wempen*

Development Editor: *Mary Cole Rack*

Manuscript Editor: *San Dee Phillips*

Cover Design: *Dan Armstrong*

Designer: *Roger Morgan*

Indexer: *Jeanne Clark*

Production Team: *Gary Adair, Katy Bodenmiller, Brad Chinn, Kim Cofer, Meshell Dinn, Mark Enochs, Stephanie Gregory, Jenny Kucera, Beth Rago, Marc Shecter, Greg Simsic, Kris Simmons, Carol Stamile, Robert Wolf*

Special thanks to C. Herbert Feltner for ensuring the technical accuracy of this book.

Screen reproductions in this book were created by means of the program Collage Plus from Inner Media, Inc., Hollis, NH.

Printed in the United States of America

Contents

1 Starting and Exiting WinFax PRO, 1

Starting WinFax PRO, 1
Getting On-Line Help, 4
Exiting WinFax PRO, 7

2 Faxing from a Windows Application, 8

Fax by Printing, 8
Setting WinFax as Your Default Printer, 13

3 Faxing from WinFax PRO, 14

Sending a Fax with WinFax, 14
Setting the Send Fax Options, 17

4 Using the Default Phonebook, 20

Creating a Phonebook Entry, 20
Selecting a Phonebook Entry, 24

5 Adding a Cover Page, 26

What Are Your Cover Page Options?, 26
Attaching a Quick Cover Page, 26
Selecting a Fancy Cover Page, 27

6 Turning Documents and Faxes into Attachments, 31

Making Documents Faxible, 31
Making Sent or Received Faxes into Attachments, 33

7 Scanning to Create an Attachment, 37

Setting Up to Scan, 37
Scanning and Sending a Document, 38
Scanning to Create an Attachment, 40

8 Sending Attachments, 42

Adding and Removing Attachments, 42
Searching for Attachments, 44
Moving Attachments, 45
Sending the Attachments, 46

9 Sending Files as Attachments, 47

Attaching Files "On-the-Fly", 47
Sending a File as a File, 49

10 Scheduling Faxes, 52

Scheduling a Fax, 52
Cancelling a Scheduled Fax, 55
Rescheduling a Fax, 55

11 Viewing and Previewing Faxes, 57

Previewing a Fax You Are About to Send, 57
Viewing Sent or Received Faxes, 58
Changing the View, 59

12 Adding Notes and Pictures to a Fax, 61

Annotating a Fax in the Viewer, 61
Adding Text Notes to a Page, 62
Adding Lines and Shapes, 65
Adding Graphic Files, 66
Selecting and Relayering Graphic Objects, 67
Cutting, Copying, and Pasting Objects, 68
Moving and Resizing Graphics, 68
Saving Your Annotations, 69

13 Tracking Fax Send Progress, 70

Viewing Outgoing Fax Information, 70
Cancelling a Fax, 72
Success or Failure?, 73

14 Resending and Forwarding a Fax, 74

Resending a Fax, 74
Forwarding a Received Fax, 75

15 Making and Selecting Your Own Phonebook, 78

Creating a Phonebook, 78
Selecting a Phonebook, 80
Adding Names and Fax Numbers, 81
Removing a Phonebook, 82

16 Advanced Phonebook Features, 83

Creating Recipient Groups, 83
Grouping in the Phonebook Window, 86
Sorting Your Phonebook Entries, 88
Searching for a Phonebook Entry, 89

17 Editing the Cover Page Contents, 91

What Does WinFax Put on Fax Pages?, 91
Changing Your User Information, 91
Changing the Fax Header, 93
Changing Cover Page Variables, 94

18 Making and Changing Cover Pages, 98

Making a New Cover Page, 98
Adding Text Boxes and Shapes to a Cover Page, 101
Changing the Look of an Object, 102

19 Receiving Faxes in Windows, 105

Turning Automatic Reception On or Off, 105
Setting the Receive Options, 106
Receiving Faxes Manually, 109

20 Viewing, Printing, and Cleaning Up a Fax, 110

Viewing and Printing Faxes, 110
Cleaning Up the Line Noise Dots, 112
Saving a Cleaned Fax, 113

21 **Turning a Fax into Editable Text, 114**

What Is Optical Character Recognition?, 114
Memory Requirements for Using OCR, 114
Setting Up to Recognize Text, 115
Recognizing Entire Pages of Text, 117
Recognizing Selected Text, 118

22 **Managing Fax Attachments, 122**

Working with the Attachments Window, 122
Creating an Attachment Folder, 123
Adding and Deleting Attachments, 125
Copying and Moving Attachments, 127
Searching for Attachments, 128

23 **Managing Fax Events, 130**

Keeping Track of Sent and Received Faxes, 130
Working with the Log Window, 131
Sorting the Send or Receive Log, 132
Deleting Fax Events, 133
Archiving Your Fax Events, 135

A **Microsoft Windows Primer, 138**

Starting Microsoft Windows, 138
Parts of a Windows Screen, 138
Using a Mouse, 140
Starting a Program, 142
Using Menus, 142
Navigating Dialog Boxes, 144
Switching Between Windows, 145
Controlling a Window, 146

B **Changing the WinFax PRO Setup, 147**

Changing the Program Setup, 147
Changing Your Fax/Modem Setup, 150
Modifying Your User Information, 154

Index, 157

Trademarks

All terms mentioned in this book that are known to be trademarks or service marks are listed below. In addition, terms suspected of being trademarks or service marks have been appropriately capitalized. Alpha Books cannot attest to the accuracy of this information. Use of a term in this book should not be regarded as affecting the validity of any trademark or service mark.

MS-DOS and Windows are trademarks, and Microsoft is a registered trademark of Microsoft Corporation.

WinFax, WinFax PRO, Cover Your Fax, Fax-a-File, and Delrina are trademarks of Delrina Technology Inc.

Introduction

You just bought a fancy, new fax modem and a copy of WinFax PRO. Your computer can now moonlight as a fax machine . . . assuming, of course, that you know what you're doing.

Now What?

You could wade through the manual that came with WinFax to find out how to perform a specific task, but that could take a while, and it might tell you more than you want to know. You need a practical guide, one that will tell you exactly how to create and send a fax, receive incoming faxes, and manage your fax files.

Welcome to the 10 Minute Guide to WinFax PRO

Because most people don't have the luxury of sitting down uninterrupted for hours at a time to learn WinFax PRO, this *10 Minute Guide* does not attempt to teach *everything* about the program. Instead, it focuses on the most often-used features. Each feature is covered in a single self-contained lesson, which is designed to take 10 minutes or less to complete.

The *10 Minute Guide* teaches you about the program without relying on technical jargon. With straightforward, easy-to-follow explanations and numbered lists that tell you what keys to press and what options to select, the *10 Minute Guide to WinFax PRO* makes learning the program quick and easy.

Who Should Use the 10 Minute Guide to WinFax PRO?

The *10 Minute Guide to WinFax PRO* is for anyone who

- Needs to learn WinFax PRO quickly.

- Feels overwhelmed or intimidated by the complexity of WinFax PRO or its documentation.

- Wants to find out quickly whether WinFax PRO will meet his or her computing needs.

- Wants a clear, concise, practical guide to the most important features of WinFax PRO.

How to Use This Book

The *10 Minute Guide to WinFax PRO* consists of a series of lessons ranging from basic startup to WinFax's more advanced features. Although you can read the book from cover to cover, you may want to skip to a specific section depending on what you want to do:

- Work with Microsoft Windows, see Appendix A.

- To install WinFax PRO, see the inside front cover of this book. If you have problems with the setup later, refer to Appendix B to learn how to change the information you entered during installation.

- To send a fax, refer to the first part of the book (Lessons 1–18). Early lessons explain how to send a quick fax. In later lessons, you learn to use the phonebook, add cover pages, create attachments, and schedule faxes.

- To receive a fax, skip ahead to Lessons 19–22. In these lessons, you learn how to receive faxes in DOS and Windows, view and print faxes, and transform fax text into text that you can edit in a word processing program.

- To work with faxes you have sent or received or attachments you have created, refer to Lessons 23 and 24.

Icons and Conventions Used in This Book

The following icons have been added throughout the book to help you find your way around:

Timesaver Tip icons offer shortcuts and hints for using the program efficiently.

Plain English icons define new terms.

Panic Button icons appear where new users often run into trouble.

The following conventions have been used to clarify the steps you must perform:

On-screen text	Any text that appears on-screen is shown in a bold type.
What you type	The information you type appears in bold color type.
Menu Names	The names of menus, commands, buttons, and dialog boxes are shown with the first letter capitalized for easy recognition.
Option selections	In any Windows application, you can select an option by using your mouse or by typing the underlined letter in the option's name. In this book, the colored letter corresponds to the underlined letter you see on-screen.

Key+Key Combinations   In many cases, you must press a two-key key combination in order to enter a command. For example, "Press Alt+X." In such cases, hold down the first key, while pressing the second key.

Lesson

Starting and Exiting WinFax PRO

In this lesson, you'll learn how to start and exit WinFax PRO and how to get on-line help.

Sending a Fax by Printing If you want to send a fax from within another Windows application (using that application's Print command), WinFax PRO does not need to be running. See Lesson 2.

Starting WinFax PRO

To use WinFax PRO, you must master some basic techniques in Microsoft Windows, including opening program group windows, running applications, dragging, and scrolling. If these terms are unfamiliar to you, refer to the Windows Primer (Appendix A) at the back of this book before moving on.

After you installed WinFax PRO (for installation instructions, see the inside front cover of this book), the installation program returned you to the Program Manager and displayed the Delrina WinFax PRO program group window as shown in Figure 1.1. This window contains the icon you will use to start WinFax PRO.

No Program Window? If you don't see the
Delrina WinFax PRO program window, open the
Program Manager's **W**indow menu, and select
Delrina WinFax PRO. If Delrina WinFax PRO is not
on the menu, click on More Windows, and select Delrina
WinFax PRO from the dialog box that appears.

To start WinFax PRO, perform the following steps:

1. Make sure your fax modem is connected and is
   turned on.

2. Do one of the following:

   - Double-click on the Delrina WinFax PRO icon.

     OR

   - Use the arrow keys to highlight the icon, and
     press Enter.

Busy COM Port? If you get a message
indicating that the COM port is busy, you prob-
ably have another telecommunications program
or on-line service software (such as CompuServe or
Prodigy) that is set up to use the modem. Exit your other
telecommunications program, and then repeat the steps
above.

This icon starts WinFax PRO.

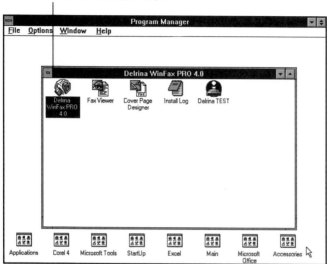

Figure 1.1   Select the Delrina WinFax PRO application icon to run the program.

The WinFax PRO opening screen appears (see Figure 1.2). You can enter commands by selecting them from the pull-down menus or by clicking on the appropriate button. The buttons under the menu bar allow you to bypass the pull-down menus for commonly used commands.

Small Windows?   If WinFax displays a tiny log window, you can click on the window's maximize button (upper right corner of the window) to enlarge it.

Button bar

Menu bar

Click here to
enlarge the window.

You can
drag
these
lines to
change
the size
of the
panes
inside
the
window.

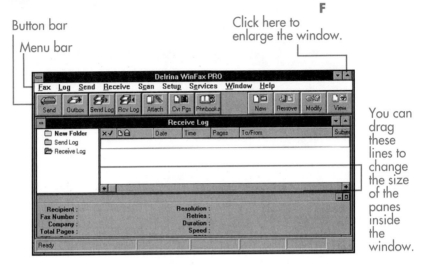

Figure 1.2   The Delrina WinFax PRO opening screen.

Getting On-Line Help

WinFax provides help for the task you are performing, as
well as for specific topics. To get help, do one of the following:

• To get help for a dialog box, display the dialog box,
and click on the Help button, or press F1.

• To get help for a menu item, highlight the item, and
press F1.

• To get help for a specific topic, open the Help
menu, and select Contents, or press F1. Click on the
topic for which you need help.

• To get help about a specific menu item or button,
press F1 to turn the mouse pointer into a help
pointer. Then click on the item or object for which
you need help.

WinFax displays a Help window like the one in Figure 1.3. You can resize the window as you can resize any window. Use the scroll bar to view any information that does not fit in the window.

Most Help windows contain terms or topics that are underlined with either a solid or dotted line. These are called *jumps*. If you click on a term with dotted underlining, WinFax displays a pop-up text box that defines the term. Click on a term or topic that is solid underlined, and WinFax displays help for the selected item.

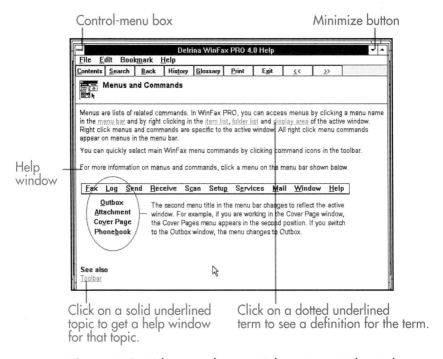

Click on a solid underlined topic to get a help window for that topic.

Click on a dotted underlined term to see a definition for the term.

Figure 1.3 When you choose a Help option, a Help window appears, covering a portion of the screen.

To move around in the Help system, click on the following buttons at the top of the Help window, or hold down the Alt key while typing the underlined character in the button's name:

Contents displays groups of Help topics.

Search allows you to search for a topic by typing the name of the topic. As you type, the cursor highlights the name of the topic that matches your entry. Keep typing until the desired topic is displayed, and then press Enter.

Back displays the previous Help screen.

History displays a list of recently accessed Help topics. This is useful if you commonly view the same Help topic.

<< displays the previous Help screen in a series of Help screens that relate to a single topic.

>> displays the next Help screen in a series of Help screens that relate to a single topic.

To exit Help, perform any of the following steps:

- Press Alt+F4, or double-click on the Control-menu box in the upper left corner of the Help window.

- Click on the Exit button.

- Click on the Minimize button in the upper right corner of the Help window to shrink the window down to an icon. This doesn't exit the Help system, it just moves it out of the way. To get the Help window back, press Ctrl+Esc, and double-click on its name.

Exiting WinFax PRO

Waiting for a Fax   If you started WinFax in order to wait for an incoming fax, do not exit the program. Simply click on the Minimize button in the upper right corner of the Delrina WinFax PRO window, or switch to another Windows application. For more details, see Lessons 19–20.

To exit WinFax and return to the Program Manager, follow these steps:

1. Press Alt+F, or click on Fax on the menu bar.

2. Press X, or click on Exit.

Quick Exit   For a quick exit, press Alt+F4, or double-click on the Control-menu box in the upper left corner of the Delrina WinFax PRO window.

Call Waiting   If you have call waiting, disable it before sending or receiving faxes. Call waiting may cause problems the fax transmissions.

In this lesson, you learned how to enter and exit WinFax and get on-line help. In the next lesson, you'll learn how to fax a document from another Windows application.

Lesson

Faxing from a Windows Application

In this lesson, you'll learn how to fax a document from a Windows application using the application's Print command.

There are two ways to fax material. If you want to send a document you created in another Windows application, you can fax it by printing it. WinFax "prints" the document to your modem, which dials the fax number and transmits the fax. If you want to combine two or more documents (for example, a document and a fax you received), you must transform the documents into *attachments* (see Lessons 6-8) and then send the fax from WinFax (as explained in Lesson 3).

> **Attachments**   Attachments are any items that are ready to fax. These include documents, databases, drawings, or spreadsheets you created and then exported into fax format; scanned images; or faxes you previously created or received. Lessons 6–8 explain how to create and send attachments.

Fax by Printing

To send a fax by printing, you must set up the application to print to WinFax (WinFax does not need to be running). The following steps explain how to send a quick fax. Later lessons explain the more advanced options, such as using a phone book, making a credit card call, and previewing and annotating the fax.

To send a quick fax:

1. Make sure your fax modem is turned on.

2. Start the Windows application you used (or will use) to create the fax document.

3. Open or create the document as you normally would.

4. Open the File menu, and select Printer Setup. A Printer Setup dialog box appears, similar to the one in Figure 2.1. With some applications, it may look different.

No Printer Setup Option?   Not all Windows applications include a Printer Setup or Select Printer command on the File menu. If you see no such option, select the Print command. When the Print dialog box appears, click on the Printer or Setup button, or a similar button.

Current default printer—

Select WinFax— as your printer.

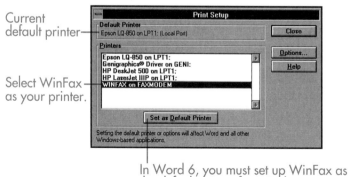

In Word 6, you must set up WinFax as the default printer for Windows.

Figure 2.1   The Printer Setup dialog box lets you choose a printer.

5. Select WinFax as your printer, and click on the OK button or its equivalent. This closes the dialog box and returns you to the Print dialog box or to your document, depending on the application.

6. If step 5 returns you to your document, open the File menu, and select Print. This displays the Print dialog box.

7. Click on the OK button. The Delrina WinFax PRO Send dialog box appears. (Your dialog box will be blank; Figure 2.2 shows a completed dialog box.)

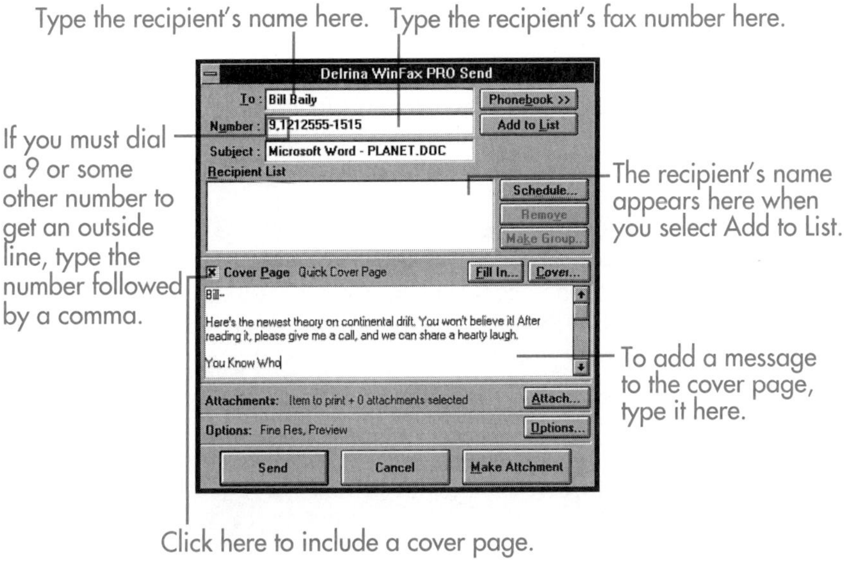
Type the recipient's name here.
Type the recipient's fax number here.
If you must dial a 9 or some other number to get an outside line, type the number followed by a comma.
The recipient's name appears here when you select Add to List.
To add a message to the cover page, type it here.
Click here to include a cover page.
Delrina WinFax PRO Send
To : Bill Baily
Number : 9,1212555-1515
Subject : Microsoft Word - PLANET.DOC
Recipient List
Phonebook >>
Add to List
Schedule...
Remove
Make Group...
Cover Page Quick Cover Page
Fill In...
Cover...
Bill--
Here's the newest theory on continental drift. You won't believe it! After reading it, please give me a call, and we can share a hearty laugh.
You Know Who
Attachments: Item to print + 0 attachments selected
Attach...
Options: Fine Res, Preview
Options...
Send
Cancel
Make Attchment

Figure 2.2 Enter the necessary information to place the call.

8. In the To Text box, type the name of the person to receive this document.

9. Press the Tab key, or click inside the **N**umber text box, and type the recipient's fax number. (Include any numbers you normally use to dial out; for example, if you have to dial 9 for an outside line, type 9, before the phone number.)

What's the Comma for?   The comma after a number tells the modem to pause before dialing the remaining numbers.

10. Click on the Add to List button. The name is added to the **R**ecipient List.

11. (Optional) To send this fax to more than one person, repeat steps 8–10.

12. (Optional) To send a cover page that includes your name, the current date and time, and the total number of pages faxed, click on the Cover Page option or press Alt+P.

Where Does the Cover Page Get Its Info?   The cover page gets the recipient's name and phone number from the To and N**u**mber text boxes. It uses the name and phone number you entered when you installed the program to identify the sender of the fax. You can change your name and phone number as explained in Lesson 17.

13. (Optional) To add text to the cover page, click inside the text box under the Cover **Page** option, and type the desired message.

14. Ignore the remaining options. Later lessons cover these more advanced features.

> **Turning Off the Preview Feature**   If you do not want to preview your fax before sending it, click on the **O**ptions button in the Send dialog box, click on Preview/Annotate, and click on OK. For more information about Send options, see Lesson 3.

15. Click on the Send button. If the Preview/Annotate option is on, the WinFax PRO Viewer appears, displaying the cover page. (Lesson 11 explains how to use the Viewer.)

16. Click on the Send Fax button. WinFax starts processing and sending the fax. The dialog box shown in Figure 2.3 displays the fax progress.

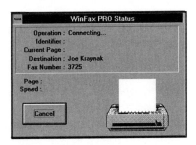

Figure 2.3   The WinFax PRO Status dialog box shows the fax progress.

Did It Work? If the fax is transmitted and received without errors, you'll get a message telling you so. If not, WinFax will try three times (once every 20 seconds). If it is unsuccessful, you can resend it. (See Lessons 13 and 14.) If you have persistent problems, Appendix B can help you determine if the modem and program are set up properly.

Setting WinFax as Your Default Printer

If you use WinFax more than you use your hard copy printer, you may want to set WinFax as your default printer. That way, you won't have to select it each time you want to print. Here's how:

1. Press Ctrl+Esc, select Program Manager, and select Switch To.

2. Open the Window menu, and select Main.

3. Double-click on the Control Panel icon.

4. Double-click on the Printers icon.

5. Select WinFax on Fax Modem from the Installed Printers list.

6. Select the Set As Default Printer option.

7. Click on the Close button.

In this lesson, you learned how to fax a document from a Windows application by using the application's Print command. In the next lesson, you will learn how to fax from WinFax PRO.

Lesson

Faxing from WinFax PRO

In this lesson, you will learn how to fax documents and attachments from WinFax PRO and how to set the Send Fax options.

The easiest way to fax a single document is to follow the steps explained in Lesson 2. Simply open the document in the Windows application you used to create it, and then print the document to WinFax. However, if you have a document that you cannot open in a Windows application, or if you want to send more than one document, you must run WinFax itself.

Which Documents? If you need to fax only a cover page with a message on it, this lesson provides all you need to know. But, if you want to send scanned images, faxes you received or sent, or documents, you must first transform these items into attachments. See Lessons 6–9.

Sending a Fax with WinFax

The following steps explain how to send a quick fax from WinFax PRO. Later lessons explain how to create and use attachments, how to use a phone book, and how to preview the fax. To send a simple fax with WinFax:

1. Make sure your fax modem is on and that WinFax PRO is running. (For help on running WinFax PRO, see Lesson 1.)

2. If WinFax PRO is not the active application, switch to it. (Press Ctrl+Esc, select Delrina WinFax PRO, and click on the Switch To button.)

3. Open the Send menu, and select Fax, or click on the Send button. The Delrina WinFax PRO Send dialog box appears, as shown in Figure 3.1. (Your dialog box will be blank; Figure 3.1 shows some information already entered.)

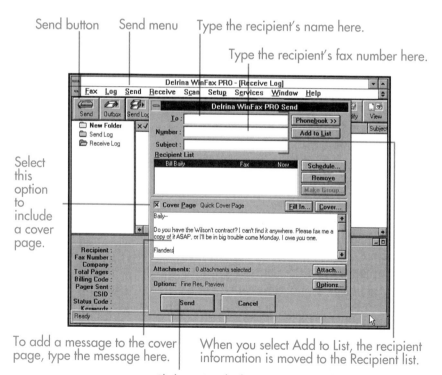

Send button   Send menu   Type the recipient's name here.

Type the recipient's fax number here.

Select this option to include a cover page.

To add a message to the cover page, type the message here.

When you select Add to List, the recipient information is moved to the Recipient list.

Click on Send when you are ready.

Figure 3.1   Enter the necessary information to place the call.

4. In the **To** text box, type the name of the person to whom you are faxing this document.

5. Press the Tab key, or click inside the **Number** text box, and type the recipient's fax number. (Include any numbers you normally use to dial out; for example, if you have to dial a 9 to get an outside line, type 9, followed by the recipient's phone number.)

> **What's the Comma for?**   The comma after a number tells the modem to pause before dialing the remaining numbers.

6. Click on the Add to List button. The name is added to the **R**ecipient List.

7. (Optional) To send this fax to more than one person, repeat steps 4–6.

8. (Optional) To send a cover page, click on the Cover Page option or press Alt+P.

> **Cover Page Info**   The default cover page is plain text, showing the recipient's name and fax number, your name and fax number, and the current date and time. To use a fancier cover page, refer to Lesson 5.

9. (Optional) To add text to the cover page, click inside the text box under the Cover **P**age option, and type a message.

10. (Optional) To send attachments, click on Attach, and use the Select Attachments dialog box to select the desired attachments. (See Lessons 6–9 to learn how to create and use attachments.)

11. (Optional) Skip ahead to the next section to learn how to set additional Send Fax options.

12. Click on the Send button. The WinFax PRO Viewer appears, displaying the cover page. (Lesson 11 describes how to use the Viewer.)

13. Click on the Send Fax button. WinFax *begins to* process and send the fax. The WinFax PRO Status dialog box appears, displaying the fax progress.

> **Successful Fax?**   If the fax is transmitted and received without errors, you'll get a message telling you so. If not, WinFax will try three times (once every 20 seconds) to send the fax. If it is unsuccessful, you can resend it. See Lessons 13 and 14. If you encounter persistent problems, refer to Appendix B to determine if your modem and the program are set up properly.

Setting the Send Fax Options

In the lower right part of the Send dialog box is an **O**ptions button that allows you to enter several preferences, including the resolution (quality) of the fax and whether you want to preview the fax before sending it. If you click on the Options button, you get the Send Options dialog box shown in Figure 3.2, where you can set the following options:

Use **Prefix**   If you have to dial a number (for example, 9) to get an outside line, turn this option on to have WinFax insert the number for you into the **Nu**mber text box. If you typed a dialing prefix in the User Setup dialog box during installation, this option is already turned on.

Credit Card To make a credit card call, select this option by placing an X in the check box.

> **Making a Credit Card Call** To make a
> credit card call, you first must specify your long-
> distance service and calling card number. Open
> the Setu**p** menu, and select Credit Card. Select
> your long distance service from the Long Distance
> Service drop-down list, and type your calling card
> number in the **C**redit Card Number text box. Click on the
> OK button.

Resolution Select Standard resolution for a lower-quality, higher speed fax transmission, or Fine for a high-quality, slower fax transmission.

Preview/Annotate WinFax is initially set to display each fax in the WinFax Viewer before sending it. To turn the Preview feature off (or back on), select Preview/Annotate.

Send Failed Pages Only If only part of a fax was transmitted successfully, you can choose this option to resend only those pages that were not transmitted.

Delete Pages After Send WinFax automatically saves the faxes you send, providing you with a record of your transmissions. To delete successfully transmitted fax pages (and save disk space), select this option.

Broadcast The Broadcast options allow you to use a new service offered by Delrina. If you have a Broadcast service account with Delrina, you can send a single fax to the service and have the service transmit the fax to up to 500 recipients. (Refer to the WinFax documentation for details.)

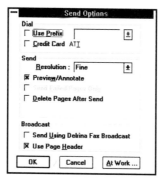

Figure 3.2 The Send Options dialog box.

In this lesson, you learned how to send a simple fax from WinFax and how to set the Send options. In the next lesson, you will learn how to add phone numbers to the WinFax phone book and select numbers from it.

Lesson

Using the Default Phonebook

4

In this lesson, you will learn how to add a name and phone number to the WinFax default phonebook, and how to select a name and number you entered.

Creating a Phonebook Entry

In the previous two lessons, you typed the name and phone number of the person you were calling. By creating a phonebook entry for a person, you can avoid typing the person's name and phone number each time. Here's how you do it:

1. Display the Delrina WinFax PRO Send dialog box. (This dialog box appears when you choose to print to WinFax or when you select the Send/Fax command in WinFax.)

2. Click on the Phonebook button. This opens a panel, as shown in Figure 4.1, that displays the phonebook options.

3. Click on the Add to Phonebook button. The New Recipient -(Default) dialog box appears, prompting you to type information for the person. (Figure 4.2 shows a sample of a completed New Recipient - (Default) dialog box.)

4. Click on the arrow to the right of the Title option, and then click on a title for the person (for example, Mr. or Ms.).

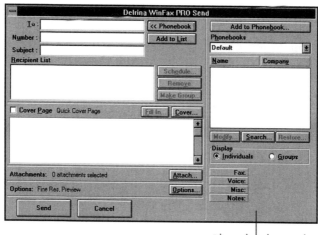

Phonebook panel

Figure 4.1 The Phonebook panel gives you access to the default phonebook.

5. Press the Tab key to move to the **First Name** text box, and type the person's first name.

6. Press the Tab key to move to the **Last** text box, and type the person's last name.

7. (Optional) Continue tabbing and typing any additional entries in the Personal Information section.

> **Mouse or Tab Key**   To move from one text box to another, either press the Tab key, or click inside the text box with the mouse. To move back one text box, press Shift+Tab. To move to a specific text box, hold down the Alt key while typing the underlined letter in the box name.

8. In the Connections section enter the following information:

Fax drop-down list: Click on the arrow to the right of this option, and select the desired type of transmission: Fax, BFT (binary file transfer), WinFax BFT, or MS At Work.

BFT and MS At Work   BFT (binary file transfer) lets you transfer a file as a file rather than as a fax. MS At Work is a new Microsoft technology that allows a PC running Windows to communicate with fax modems, photocopiers, and large public network services. To perform a binary file transfer, see Lesson 9, "Sending Files As Attachments."

Country   To dial an overseas number, type the country code here. (You can find country codes in a phone book such as the Yellow Pages.)

Area   If you are calling a long-distance number, enter the required area code here.

Long-Distance and International Calls   WinFax "assembles" a phone number by using information from two sources: the phonebook entry and the User Setup dialog box. For example, if you enter an area code that differs from your area code, WinFax inserts the long-distance access number (1) before the area code whenever you select the long-distance recipient from the phonebook. To check your user setup information, refer to Appendix B.

Local Number   Enter the recipient's fax number here.

Extension   If you must dial an extension to connect with the recipient's fax machine (and you can dial the extension without operator assistance), type the required extension here.

Voice and Fax Numbers   The numbers in
the Fax row are for dialing a fax machine. The
numbers in the Voice row are for making voice
calls (to talk to the person). The voice numbers are
optional.

9. (Optional) If you send documents different ways
   (by fax or MCI mail) from different locations (home
   or office), then use the drop-down lists in the Send
   By section to select a transmission method for each
   location.

10. Press Enter, or click on the OK button. You are
    returned to the Send dialog box, and the new entry
    appears in the phone list.

You must enter a first name, last
name, or company name. All other
personal information is optional.

New Recipient - [Default]

Personal Information
Title: Ms.   First Name: Alexandra   Last: Pinkerton
Company: Pinkerton's International
Address1: 11711 North Wabash
Address2:
City: Chicago   State/Country : IL   Zip Code: 60601
Notes:
Billing: Misc:

Connections
Country Area Local Number   Extension
Fax   1   312   555-5555   x
Voice: x

Send From
Home: Fax   Away: Fax   Office: Fax

[OK]   [Cancel]

You must enter
a fax number.   Voice numbers
are optional.

Figure 4.2   The New Recipient dialog box lets you create a
phonebook entry.

Editing an Entry You can edit a phonebook entry at any time. Go to the Send Fax dialog box phone list, highlight the entry, and then click on the Modify button.

Make Your Own Phonebook When you add names to a phonebook, you are adding them to WinFax's default phonebook. You can also create your own phonebook and add numbers to it as explained in Lesson 15.

Selecting a Phonebook Entry

Once you add a person's name and phone number as a phonebook entry, you can select the name from the phonebook at any time. WinFax retrieves all the information necessary to place the call. Select a name from the phonebook as follows:

1. Display the Delrina WinFax PRO Send dialog box. (This dialog box appears when you choose to print to WinFax or when you select the Send/Fax command in WinFax.)

2. If necessary, click on the Phonebook button to display the phonebook panel.

3. From the list of names, select the person you want to send the fax to. See Figure 4.3.

4. Perform any other steps required to send the fax.

When you select a recipient from the list, WinFax inserts the recipient's name and fax number in the appropriate fields.

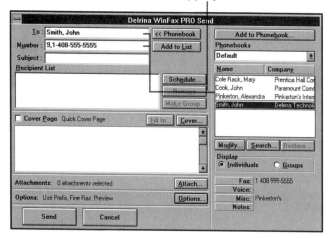

Figure 4.3 Select a person's name from the list.

In this lesson, you learned how to add a person's name and fax number to the phonebook and how to select a phonebook entry. In the next lesson, you will learn how to add a cover page.

Lesson

Adding a Cover Page

In this lesson, you will learn how to select a cover page and how to change the information about you that appears on the cover page.

What Are Your Cover Page Options?

WinFax gives you two cover page options: Quick Cover Page and Cover Your Fax. The Quick Cover Page is a no-nonsense cover page that includes today's date and time, your name, and any additional information you want to type. Cover Your Fax provides a collection of fancier cover pages that include graphics, lines, and fancy type. In this lesson, you will learn how to use both types of cover pages.

Attaching a Quick Cover Page

If you followed the instructions in Lessons 2 and 3 for sending a fax, you may have sent a Quick Cover Page already. When you enter the **Send/Fax** command (or print a document to WinFax), you get the Send dialog box, as shown in Figure 5.1. After addressing the fax, you can click on the Cover **Page** option, which is set up initially for a Quick Cover Page. You can then type a message in the text box that's below the Cover **Page** option.

WinFax uses the Quick Cover Page by default.

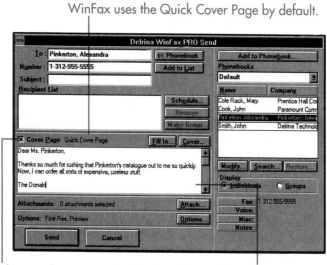

Make sure there is an x in this check box. Type your message here.

Figure 5.1   A Quick Cover Page is easy to send.

Selecting a Fancy Cover Page

WinFax comes with a program called Cover Your Fax, a
cover page designer that includes several predesigned cover
pages. To learn how to design a cover page, see Lessons 17
and 18. To select a cover page, do the following:

1. Display the Delrina WinFax PRO Send dialog box.
   (The dialog box that appears when you choose to
   print to WinFax or when you select the Send/Fax
   command in WinFax.)

2. Click on the Cover button, or press Alt+C. The
   Select Cover Page dialog box appears. Figure 5.2
   shows the Select Cover Page dialog box with a
   cover page selected.

Select a collection of cover pages.

Select Show All to see pictures of all the cover pages in the group.

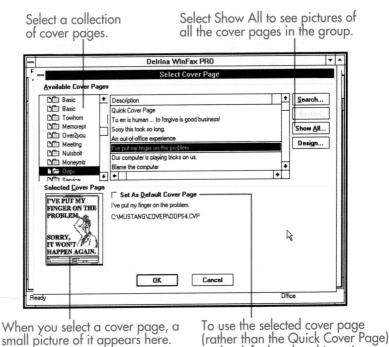

When you select a cover page, a small picture of it appears here.

To use the selected cover page (rather than the Quick Cover Page) as the default, select this option.

Figure 5.2 WinFax comes with several collections of cover pages.

3. From the Available Cover Pages list, double-click on the file you think has the cover pages you want. Each file in the list contains several cover pages. The Description list displays the names of the cover pages.

4. From the Description list (the list that has the names of the cover pages), click on the cover page you want. A sketch of it appears in the Selected Cover Page area. (If a cover page description does not say "fill-in area," you cannot type a message on it.)

Display More Cover Pages To see more of the cover pages in the selected library, choose the Show All button. A window appears, showing up to eight cover pages. Use the scroll bar to see additional cover pages in the group. To select a cover page, double-click on it.

5. (Optional) To make this cover page the default (instead of the Quick Cover Page), select Set as Default Cover Page.

6. Click on the OK button. WinFax returns you to the Send Fax dialog box. The name of the selected cover page appears to the right of the Cover Page option.

7. Make sure there is a check mark in the Cover Page check box.

8. To add text to the cover page, click inside the text box under the Cover Page option, and type the desired message.

Using the Fill In Button You can also add a message to the cover page by clicking on the Fill In button. This displays the cover page in the Cover Page Filler, which shows the cover page as it will appear on the recipient's fax machine. Type your message, and then open the File menu, and select Send Fax, or click on the Send Fax button. You can use options from the Text menu to style and spell-check your text.

9. Perform any other steps required to send the fax.

Changing the Cover Page User Information
WinFax inserts your name, the current date and
time, and the page number at the top of the cover
page and inserts additional information at the
bottom of the page. To control the position and content of
this information, see Lesson 17.

In this lesson, you learned how to select a Quick Cover
Page and a fancy Cover Your Fax cover page. For more control
over cover pages, see Lessons 17 and 18. In the next lesson,
you will learn how to turn existing documents and faxes into
attachments that you can fax.

Lesson

Turning Documents and Faxes into Attachments

In this lesson, you will learn how to transform documents you created and faxes you sent or received into attachments that you can fax.

Documents WinFax considers any file you create to be a document. These include graphic images, spreadsheets, word processing documents, databases, and other files.

Making Documents Faxible

There are two ways to fax a document that you have created in a Windows application: You can print the document to WinFax PRO (see Lesson 2), or convert the document into an attachment (as explained here) and then fax the attachment (see Lesson 9). To transform a document into an attachment, do the following:

1. Start the Windows application you used (or will use) to create the fax document.

2. Open or create the document as usual.

Save Your Work   If you create the document, be sure to save it to disk as you normally do.

3. Make sure the program is set up to use WinFax PRO as the printer. (For details, see Lesson 2.)

4. If you are back in your document, open the File menu, and select Print. This displays the Print dialog box.

5. Click on the OK button. The Delrina WinFax PRO Send dialog box appears.

6. Click on the Make Attachment button at the bottom of the Send dialog box. The Create Attachment dialog box appears. Figure 6.1 shows a completed dialog box.

Initially, WinFax inserts the application name and document file name, but you can type your own description.

Keywords are optional.

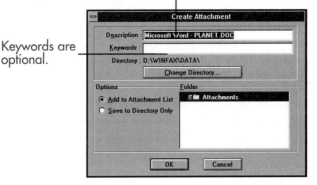

Figure 6.1   The Create Attachment dialog box.

7. (Optional) If desired, type or edit a description in the Description text box. The description will appear in the list of fax attachments, as explained in Lesson 8.

8. (Optional) In the **K**eywords text box, type any words that will help you find this attachment later.

9. (Optional) To save the attachment in a directory other than the one shown on the Directory line, click on the Change Directory button. Then select the desired drive from the **D**rives list and a directory from the **D**irectories list, and click on OK.

10. In the Options group, make sure the **A**dd to Attachment List check box has a check mark in it. (The **S**ave to Directory Only option prevents the attachment from appearing in the Attachment list, which may make it difficult to find later.)

> **Attachment Folders** The **F**older list in the Options group lets you save the attachment in a folder that keeps attachments together. To learn how to create and use folders, see Lesson 22.

11. Click on the OK button. WinFax converts the document into an attachment and saves it to disk. (Fax attachment files are assigned the extension **.FXS**.)

You are returned to the application you used to create the document. To fax the attachment you just created, see Lesson 8.

Making Sent or Received Faxes into Attachments

If you send or receive a fax and later decide you want to send it to someone else, you should first transform the sent or received fax into an attachment. Here's how:

1. Change to the WinFax PRO program window, if necessary.

2. Click on one of the following buttons:

   Send Log   To view a list of faxes you sent.

   Rcv Log   To view a list of faxes you received.

   The Send Log or Receive Log window appears.
   Figure 6.2 shows the Receive Log window.

You can click on the Send Log or Rcv Log button, or double-click
on the desired folder.

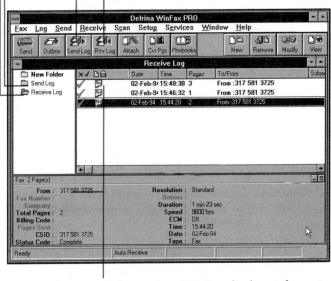

When you click on a fax, WinFax displays information about it.

Figure 6.2 The Receive Log window displays records of
received faxes.

3. Click on the fax you want to transform into an
   attachment, or use the down arrow key to highlight it.

4. Click on the View button. The selected fax is
   displayed in the Viewer.

5. Open the File menu, and select Export. The Export dialog box appears. Figure 6.3 shows a completed Export dialog box.

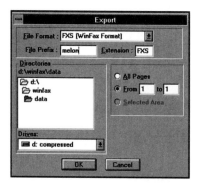

Figure 6.3 A Completed Export dialog box.

6. From the File Format drop-down list, select FXS (WinFax Format).

7. Select File Prefix, and type a file name prefix for the file (up to five characters). (WinFax uses the last three characters of the standard eight-character file name for page numbers: 001, 002, 003, and so on.)

8. Use the Drives and Directories lists to specify the drive and directory where you want the attachment file saved.

9. In the pages group, specify which pages you want to convert into an attachment:

   All Pages converts all the pages.

   From...to... converts a range of pages. Type the page numbers to specify the range.

   Selected Area converts the selected area into an attachment (assuming you selected an area).

Sending Sent or Received Faxes On-the-Fly You don't have to convert a sent or received fax into an attachment before sending it (see Lesson 9). However, by transforming a fax into an attachment, you make it easier to combine attachments later.

10. Click on the OK button, or press Enter. WinFax converts the specified pages into attachments and displays the last page it converted.

11. Open the File menu, and click on Exit to leave the Viewer. You can now fax the attachments you created, as explained in Lesson 8.

In this lesson, you learned how to turn documents and previously sent or received faxes into attachments that you can fax. In the next lesson, you will learn how to scan a paper document to create an attachment. If you do not have a scanner, skip Lesson 7.

Lesson

Scanning to Create an Attachment

In this lesson, you will learn how to scan a paper document or image into WinFax to create an attachment or to send the scan immediately.

Setting Up to Scan

If you have a Twain-compatible scanner connected to your computer, you can scan an image into WinFax and send the scanned image immediately, or you can save it as an attachment to send later.

> **Twain-Compatible**   Twain is the standard with which most new scanners comply. To determine if your scanner is Twain-compatible, check the documentation that came with it.

Before you try to scan in WinFax, take the following steps to set up your scanner and scanning software:

1. Make sure your scanner is connected, your scanning software is installed, and the scanner is on (if your scanner has an on/off switch).

Hand-Held Scanner Most hand-held scanners have a button you must hold down while
scanning. If you have such a scanner, don't worry
about the on/off switch.

2. Set the scanner to black-and-white, line drawing or
   text mode. (You cannot scan in color or in shades
   of gray.)

3. Set the scanner to 200-by-200 dpi (dots per inch).

   Once your scanner is set up, you can scan and send a
document or scan the document and save it as an attachment
file to send later.

What Can You Scan? With your scanner set
to black-and-white line drawing at 200-by-200
dpi, you will get a low-resolution, black-and-white
scan. If you scan photos or color or shaded
artwork, the image will appear in black-and-white: no
color and no shading.

Scanning and Sending a Document

To scan a document and send it immediately, do the following:

1. If you have a table scanner, load the page you want
   to scan into the scanner, as you normally would.

2. Open the Scan menu (in the WinFax PRO program
   window), and select Scan and Send. The Scanner
   program window appears. This window differs
   depending on your scanner. See Figure 7.1.

As you scan, the
image appears here.

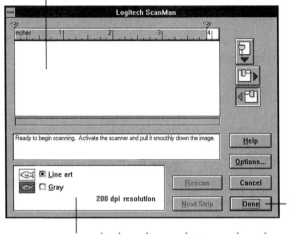

Click on
the Done
button
If your scan program displays the resolution and mode   or its
settings, make sure they are set to line art and 200 dpi.   equivalent

Figure 7.1   A sample scanner program window.

3. If your scanner displays a preview image for adjusting your scanner, perform any steps required to
enhance the appearance of the image.

4. Perform any steps as usual to scan the image. For
example, if you have a hand-held scanner, you may
have to drag the scanner over the image and then
click on the Done, Final, or Scan button in the
program window.

> **More Pages?**   If you have an autofeed
> mechanism on your scanner, WinFax will scan all
> the pages you loaded. If you have to feed your
> scanner manually, or if you are using a hand-held
> scanner, you'll get a dialog box asking if you want to
> scan another page.

5. A dialog box may appear asking if you want to scan another page. Select Yes and repeat step 4, or select No. When you select No, the WinFax Send Fax dialog box appears.

6. Perform the steps necessary to send the fax.

Scanning to Create an Attachment

If you want to combine scanned pages with other attachments, you should save the scanned page(s) as an attachment. Here's how:

1. If you have a table scanner, load the page you want to scan into the scanner, as you normally would. (If you have a hand-held scanner, skip this step.)

2. Open the Scan menu (in the WinFax PRO program window), and select Scan and File. The Scanner program window appears. See Figure 7.1.

3. If your scanner displays a preview image for adjusting your scanner, take the necessary steps to adjust the scanner.

4. Follow the usual procedures to scan the image. For example, if you have a hand-held scanner, you may have to drag the scanner over the image and then click on the Done, Final, or Scan button in the program window.

5. If a dialog box appears asking if you want to scan another page, select the desired option. When the scanning is complete, the Create Attachment dialog box appears, as shown in Figure 7.2.

You can type your own description or use the one WinFax suggests.

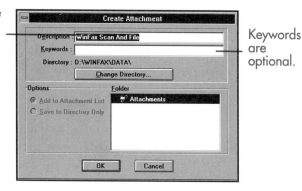

Keywords are optional.

Figure 7.2 Save the scanned document as an attachment.

6. (Optional) Type or edit the description of the document in the Description text box. This description will appear in the list of fax attachments, as explained in Lesson 9.

7. (Optional) Tab to the Keywords text box, and enter any words that will help you find this attachment later.

8. (Optional) To save the attachment in a directory of your choice, click on the Change Directory button, select the desired drive from the Drives list and a directory from the Directories list, and click on OK.

9. Click on the OK button. WinFax converts the document into an attachment and saves it to disk. (Fax attachment files are assigned the extension **.FXS**.)

To send the scanned document or image that you just transformed into an attachment, see Lesson 8.

In this lesson, you learned how to use your scanner to create a faxible document to send now or later. In the next lesson, you will learn how to fax any attachments you have created.

Lesson

Sending Attachments

In this lesson, you will learn how to send the attachments you created in Lessons 6 and 7.

Adding and Removing Attachments

To send an attachment, you select it from a list of attachments you created. Here's how you do it:

1. Display the Delrina WinFax PRO Send dialog box. (This dialog box appears when you choose to print to WinFax or when you select the Send/Fax command in WinFax.)

The attachments you created appear here.

Select an attachment, and click on the Add to Send List button.

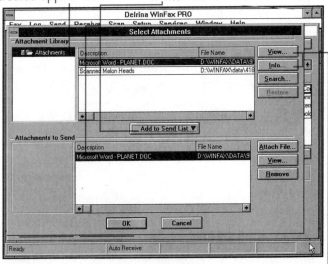

Use the View or Information button to see the selected attaachments.

Figure 8.1 The Select Attachments dialog box.

2. Click on the Attach button, or press Alt+A. The Select Attachments dialog box appears, as shown in Figure 8.1.

3. In the Attachment Library list, click on the desired attachment, or use the down arrow key to highlight it.

4. To view the selected attachment, click on the View or Info button. The View button displays the attachment in the Viewer; to leave the Viewer, open the File menu, and select Exit. The Info button displays a thumbnail view of the attachment. When you're done viewing, click on the Close button.

Can't Find Your Attachment? If you don't see your attachment in the list, you can click on the Search button and search for it by description, keywords, or file name. The procedure is explained later in this lesson.

5. Click on the Add to Send List button, or press Alt+L.

6. (Optional) Repeat steps 3–5 to add more attachments.

7. (Optional) To remove an attachment, click on the attachment in the Attachments to Send list, and then click on the Remove button.

Attachment Folders You can create folders for organizing your attachments. To learn how to create and use folders, and how to delete and rearrange attachments, see Lesson 22.

Searching for Attachments

If you have a long list of available attachments, finding the right one can be difficult. However, WinFax allows you to search for a specific attachment or group of attachments by file name, description, or keywords (assuming you assigned keywords to the attachment). To search using any of this information, take the following steps:

1. In the Select Attachments dialog box, click on the Search button. The Search Attachments dialog box appears, as shown in Figure 8.2.

2. Enter information in one or more of the text boxes:

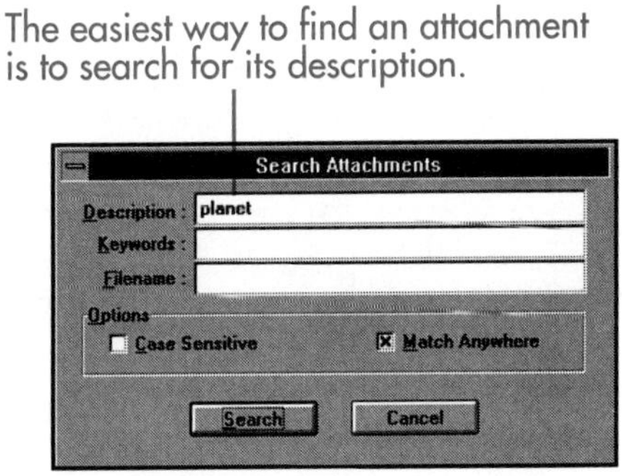

The easiest way to find an attachment is to search for its description.

Figure 8.2 Use the Search Attachments dialog box to look for your attachments.

- To search the attachment descriptions, type the text you want to search for in the Description text box.

- To search for keywords you assigned to the attachments, type the keyword text in the Keywords text box. (You can search for keywords only if you assigned keywords to the attachment when you created it.)

- To search for an attachment by file name, type the file name in the Filename text box.

Weird File Names   When you create an attachment, WinFax assigns it a random number, making it nearly impossible to recognize a file by name. You can search more effectively by looking for the attachment by its description.

•To have WinFax distinguish between uppercase and lowercase entries, select **Case Sensitive**.

Case Sensitive Searches   With **C**ase Sensitive on, if you search for "Account," WinFax will skip over "account" and "AC-COUNT." With **C**ase Sensitive off, if you search for "Account," WinFax will find "Account," "account," and "ACCOUNT."

* To have WinFax locate your search text no matter where it appears in the Keyword or Description entry, select Match Anywhere. With **Match Anywhere** off, WinFax expects to find the search text at the beginning of the entry.

3. Select Search. WinFax returns you to the Select Attachments dialog box and displays a list of attachments that match your search instructions.

4. To return the full list of available attachments, click on the Restore button.

Moving Attachments

Attachments are added to the outgoing fax in the order in which you added them. You can rearrange the attachments by taking the following steps:

1. In the Attachments to Send list, move the mouse pointer over the attachment you want to move.

2. Hold down the mouse button, and drag the mouse pointer up or down in the list. The mouse pointer appears as a double horizontal line that you can move to the top or bottom of the list or between two other attachments.

3. Release the mouse button. The attachment is repositioned.

Sending the Attachments

After you have selected and arranged all the attachments you want to send, click on the OK button. This returns you to the Send Fax dialog box. Perform any steps normally required to send the fax.

In this lesson, you learned how to include attachments in an outgoing fax. In the next lesson, you will learn how to create and send attachments "on-the-fly" and how to send files.

9

Sending Files as Attachments

In this lesson, you will learn how to send files that have not been transformed into attachments.

WinFax 4 introduces two new features that let you send files you have not yet transformed into attachments. You can have WinFax automatically transform a file into an attachment on-the-fly, or you can perform a binary file transfer that sends the file without converting it into an attachment. The following sections tell you how to use both features.

Binary File Transfer   You can perform a binary file transfer only if both your modem and the recipient's modem support binary file transfers. Check your modem documentation, and have the recipient check his or her documentation before attempting a binary file transfer. Or you can try it, and if it doesn't work, you'll know you can't do it.

Attaching Files "On-the-Fly"

In Lessons 6-8, you created attachments and then selected the ones to send. Another way to create an attachment is to select the file you want to attach, and have WinFax do all the busy work. WinFax runs the program used to create the file, transforms the file into an attachment, and then attaches the file to your outgoing fax. Here's how:

1. Display the Delrina WinFax PRO Send dialog box.

2. Click on the Attach button, or press Alt+A. The Select Attachments dialog box appears.

3. Click on the Attach File button. The Select Attachment Files dialog box appears, as shown in Figure 9.1.

> **Not Just Any File** The file you select must be a file that can be opened in one of your Windows applications and can be transformed into a graphics file. For example, you cannot send a program file (.EXE or .COM) or a sound file (.WAV). You can send fax files that you have sent (FXD files) or received (FXR files) without transforming them into attachments.

Select the file you want to send.

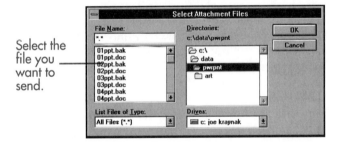

Figure 9.1 Use the Select Attachment Files dialog box to select the file you want to send.

4. Select the drive, directory, and file name of the file you want to send.

5. Click on the OK button. You return to the Select Attachments dialog box.

6. Add more attachments, if desired, and then click on the OK button. You return to the Send dialog box.

7. Perform any remaining steps required to send the fax, and then click on the Send button. The Attachment Image Creation dialog box appears.

WinFax runs the program used to create the file, transforms the file into an attachment, attaches the file to your outgoing fax, dials the recipient's number, and transmits the fax.

Sending a File as a File

Attachments (even text-based attachments) are graphics files—collections of tiny dots that act as a picture. If the recipient has WinFax, the recipient can display and edit the fax as a graphics file, but cannot open the file in a word processing or spreadsheet program. If you want to send a document, spreadsheet, graphics, or sound file that the recipient can open and edit, you can send it as a binary file. To send a binary file, you must first create or edit the phonebook entry for the recipient to specify binary file transfer. Here's what you do:

1. Display the Delrina WinFax PRO Send dialog box. (This dialog box appears when you choose to print to WinFax or when you select the Send/Fax command in WinFax.)

2. Click on the Phonebook button, if necessary, to open the phonebook panel.

3. Click on the Add to Phonebook button, or highlight an existing phonebook entry and click on the Modify button. The New Recipient or Modify Recipient dialog box appears.

4. Type the required information, as explained in Lesson 4.

5. In the Connections drop-down list, select the BFT (Binary File Transfer) or WinFax BFT option. (See Figure 9.2.)

6. Click on the Programs button. The Programs Available dialog box appears, as shown in Figure 9.2.

Available Programs WinFax needs to know which software the recipient has to determine which files can or cannot be used by the recipient. The Programs Available dialog box allows you to indicate which programs the recipient has.

7. The Possible Programs list displays the programs from which you can select. Click on one to choose it, and then click on the Add button to copy the program to the Available At Recipient list.

8. Click on the OK button to return to the New or Modify Record dialog box.

9. Click on OK to add your changes to the phonebook and return to the Send Fax dialog box.

Use the Add button to copy a program from the Possible to Available list.

```
┌──────────────────────────────────────────────────────────────┐
│ ▭  ▭              Modify Recipient - [Default]                 │
│ Fi  Personal Information                                       │
│  ▭       Title: Mr.    ± First Name: John    Last: Cook       │
│      Company: Paramount Communications                         │
│      Address1:                                                 │
│      Address2:                                                 │
│ I       City:           State/Country :        Zip Code:      │
│        Notes:                                                  │
│       Billing:                    Misc: Paramount Communications│
│ ┌    Connections                                               │
│           Country  Area    Local Number      Extension         │
│      BFT    ± 1     317     556-3646      x        Programs... │
│   ▭                  Programs Available                        │
│              Select the programs that the recipient has.       │
│       This is used to decide which type of files can be sent without being converted to a fax.│
│      Possible Programs              Available At Recipient      │
│ A    1-2-3 Worksheet(123w.exe)  ▲  ┌─ Add ▶▶ ─┐ 1-2-3 Worksheet(123w.exe) ▲│
│      aldsetup.exe                               aldsetup.exe   │
│ [    Calendar File(calendar.exe)                Calendar File(calendar.exe)│
│      Card File(cardfile.exe)                    Card File(cardfile.exe)│
│      graph5.exe                                 graph5.exe     │
│      Media Player(mplayer.exe)                  Media Player(mplayer.exe)│
│      Microsoft Access 2.0 Database(msac ▼       Microsoft Access 2.0 Database(msac ▼│
│ Re           ┌────OK────┐  ┌─Cancel─┐                          │
└──────────────────────────────────────────────────────────────┘
```

Make sure BFT appears here.

The Programs button displays the Programs Available dialog box.

Figure 9.2 You must tell WinFax that you want to perform a binary file transfer to the recipient.

Now that you have your recipient set up to receive a binary file, you can send the file as an attachment:

1. Complete the Send dialog box, as usual.

2. Click on the Attach button, or press Alt+A. The Select Attachments dialog box appears, as in Figure 8.1.

3. Click on the Attach File button. The Select Attachment Files dialog box appears (the same dialog box shown in Figure 9.1).

4. Select the drive, directory, and file name of the file you want to send.

5. Click on the OK button. You return to the Select Attachments dialog box.

6. Click on the OK button. You return to the Send dialog box.

7. Perform any remaining steps required to send the fax, and then click on the Send button.

> **ASSOCINCOMPLETE**   If you get the **ASSOCINCOMPLETE** message, you may not have specified BFT or selected the appropriate program for your recipient. Repeat the first set of steps in this section, and make sure the recipient information is correct. If you run into other problems, try WinFax BFT rather than BFT.

In this lesson, you learned how to send files as attachments "on-the-fly" and how to perform a binary file transfer. In the next lesson, you will learn how to schedule your faxes to send at a more convenient or less expensive time.

Lesson

Scheduling Faxes

In this lesson, you will learn how to schedule your faxes to have WinFax send them at a more convenient or less expensive time.

Scheduling a Fax

WinFax normally sends a fax immediately after you click on the Send button in the Send dialog box. To send a fax on a scheduled day or time, perform the following steps:

1. Display the Delrina WinFax PRO Send dialog box. (This dialog box appears when you choose to print to WinFax or when you select the Send/Fax command in WinFax.)

2. Address the fax to one or more recipients as usual.

3. In the **Recipient** List, select the people to whom you want to send the fax at a scheduled time.

> **Multiple Recipients** To select two or more recipients who are not next to each other in the list, hold down the Ctrl key while clicking on each person's name. To select neighboring names, click on the first name and then hold down the Shift key while clicking on the last name.

4. Click on the Schedule button. The Schedule/Modify Events dialog box appears, as shown in Figure 10.1.

Select a transmission method.

Make sure
Schedule or Off
Peak is selected.

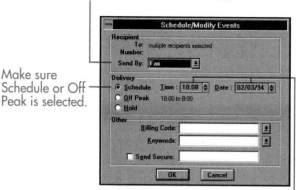

Specify a date and time.

Figure 10.1   The Schedule/Modify Events dialog box.

5. From the Send By drop-down list, select the desired method of transmission. (This is usually Fax, but you may want to send a binary file (BFT) or send by electronic mail.)

6. Make sure the Schedule option is selected.

7. Select the Date or Time option, click on the number you want to change, and type the desired number. When you click on a number, a triangle appears below it. You can then type a number or use the arrow buttons to the right of the option to increase or decrease the number.

8. Repeat step 7 until the desired date and time are displayed.

9. Click on the OK button.

10. (Optional) Repeat steps 3–9 if needed, to schedule the fax for other people in the Recipient List.

11. Perform any other steps required to send the fax, and then click on the Send button.

When you schedule a fax, the fax is added to the
Outbox list, as shown in Figure 10.2. To view this list, open
the Fax menu, and select Outbox, or click on the Outbox
button in the button bar.

Click on this button to display the **O**utbox list.

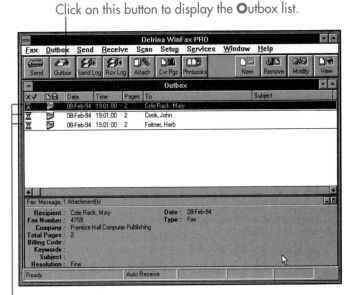

Scheduled faxes

Figure 10.2   When you schedule a fax, it is listed as a
scheduled event.

WinFax Must Be Running   If WinFax is not
running on the scheduled date and at the scheduled time, WinFax cannot send the fax automatically, so make sure you leave your computer and
WinFax running. If WinFax is not running at the scheduled time, the fax will be sent the next time you run
WinFax.

Cancelling a Scheduled Fax

If you decide later that you do not want to send a scheduled fax, you can remove it from the Outbox list. Here's how:

1. Select the scheduled fax you want to remove in the Outbox list.

2. Click on the Remove button, or open the Outbox menu and select Remove. A dialog box appears, prompting you to confirm.

3. Click on Yes to remove the fax or No to keep it at the scheduled time.

> **Quick Right-Click Commands** Whenever you are working with a list of items, you can right-click on an item in the list to display a pop-up menu of available commands. For example, to remove an item from the Outbox list, right-click on the item, and click on Remove.

Rescheduling a Fax

If you schedule a fax and later decide to send the fax on a different date or time, you can reschedule it as follows:

1. Select the fax to reschedule in the Outbox list.

2. To change the scheduled time, open the Outbox menu, and select Reschedule. The Schedule dialog box appears, showing the scheduled date and time.

3. Select the Date or Time option, click on the number you want to change, and type the new number. When you click on a number, a triangle appears below it. You can then type a number or use the arrow keys to the right of the option to increase or decrease the number.

4. Repeat step 3 for any other settings you want to change.

5. Click on the OK button.

6. (Optional) To send the fax to a different recipient, open the Outbox menu, and choose Change Destination. The Change Destination dialog box appears.

   Change the recipient name in the To box and the recipient's number in the Number box.

7. Click on the OK button.

> **Sending Faxes Now**   To send a scheduled fax now, select the fax, and then pull down the Outbox menu, and select Send Now. The Schedule menu also contains commands for holding scheduled faxes (to prevent them from being sent at the scheduled time), and for releasing faxes that you have put on hold.

In this lesson, you learned how to schedule a fax, cancel a scheduled fax, and reschedule a fax. In the next lesson, you will learn how to preview a fax before sending it.

Lesson

Viewing and Previewing Faxes

In this lesson, you will learn how to view a fax you sent or received, and preview a fax you are about to send.

Previewing a Fax You Are About to Send

You can preview the cover page and attachments you are about to send by turning on the Preview feature. With Preview on, when you send a fax, WinFax runs the Fax Viewer and displays the fax you just created. To turn the Preview feature on, perform the following steps:

1. Display the Delrina WinFax PRO Send dialog box. (This dialog box appears when you choose to print to WinFax or when you select the Send/Fax command in WinFax.)

2. Click on the Options button. The Send Options dialog box appears, as shown in Figure 11.1.

3. Click on Preview/Annotate, or press Alt+W. An **X** appears in the check box, showing that the feature is on.

4. Click on the OK button. You are returned to the Send Fax dialog box.

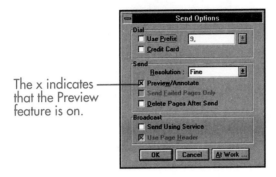

The x indicates that the Preview feature is on.

Figure 11.1   The Send Options dialog box lets you turn the Preview feature on or off.

With the Preview feature on, WinFax displays each fax you send in the Viewer before sending it. To flip pages in the Viewer, click on the Previous Page or Next Page button (see Figure 11.2). To leave the Viewer, click on the Send Fax button, or open the File menu, and select Exit.

Viewing Sent or Received Faxes

In addition to previewing faxes you are about to send, you can use the Fax Viewer to look at faxes you have sent or received. To view a fax you sent, perform the following steps:

1. Open the Send menu, and select Log, or click on the Send Log button in the button bar. A list of the faxes you sent appears in the Send Log list.

2. Click on the fax whose pages you want to view. Thumbnail pictures of the fax appear at the bottom of the window. (If the thumbnails are not displayed, open the Window menu, and select Display Thumbnails.)

   • To view a specific page in the Viewer, double-click on the thumbnail view of the page.

- To display the first page, click on the View button in the button bar.

- To flip pages in the Viewer, click on the Previous Page or Next Page button.

3. To leave the Viewer, open the File menu, and select Exit.

You view a fax you received in much the same way that you view a fax you sent:

1. Open the Receive menu, and select Log, or click on the Rcv Log button in the button bar. A list of the faxes you received appears in the Receive Log list.

2. Click on the fax whose pages you want to view. Thumbnail pictures of the fax appear at the bottom of the window. (If the thumbnails are not displayed, open the Window menu, and select Display Thumbnails.)

   - To view a specific page in the Viewer, double-click on its thumbnail view.

   - To display the first page, click on the View button in the button bar.

   - To flip pages in the Viewer, click on the Previous Page or Next Page button.

3. To leave the Viewer, open the File menu, and select Exit.

Changing the View

No matter how you choose to view your fax, it appears in the Viewer as shown in Figure 11.2. You can change the display size of the fax by selecting a size from the View menu or by clicking on the view buttons as shown. To flip from one page to the next or previous one, use the page buttons.

Use these buttons to magnify a section of the page.

Use these buttons to increase or decrease the size of the page as displayed.

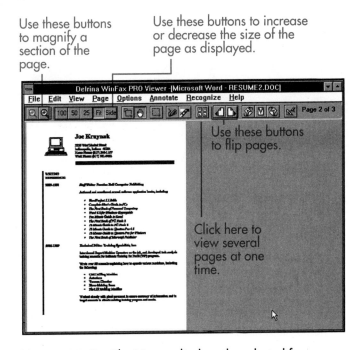

Use these buttons to flip pages.

Click here to view several pages at one time.

Figure 11.2 The Viewer displays the selected fax.

In this lesson, you learned how to view a fax you have sent or received, or preview a fax you are about to send. In the next lesson, you will learn how to add text and pictures to a fax page.

Lesson 12

Adding Notes and Pictures to a Fax

In this lesson, you will learn how to add text and graphics to a fax page that you are about to send.

Annotating a Fax in the Viewer

Sometimes, you may want to add notes or pictures to a fax attachment or fill out a form before sending it. You can do all this in the Viewer. Before you can add text and graphics to a fax, however, you must display the ribbon that contains the tools you need. Take the following steps:

1. Display the fax you want to annotate in the Viewer. (Look back at Lesson 11 for details.)

2. Open the Annotate menu.

3. Select Show. The ribbon appears as shown in Figure 12.1.

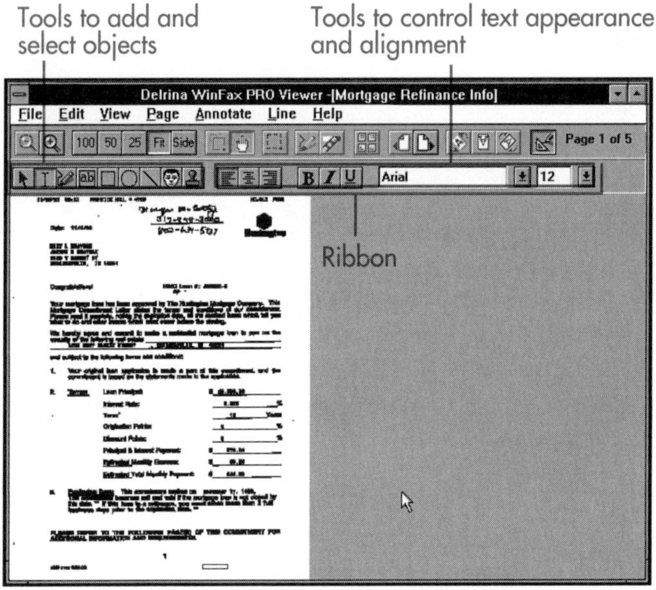

Tools to add and
select objects

Tools to control text appearance
and alignment

Figure 12.1 The ribbon contains a toolbar and text formatting controls.

Adding Text Notes to a Page

To add text to a page, you must put it in a text box. Here's how:

1. Click on the Text tool (the button with the **ab** on it).

2. Move the mouse pointer where you want the upper left corner of the box to appear.

3. Hold down the mouse button, and drag the pointer to where you want the lower right corner of the box to appear.

4. Release the mouse button. The text box appears with a blinking insertion point inside.

5. Type your text.

6. Click outside the box when you are done.

> **Editing Text Later**   To edit the text you typed, click on the text box, and then click on the Text Editing tool (the button with the I-beam on it). Move the mouse pointer where you want to type, and click the left mouse button.

To change the text box line thickness, open the Line menu, and choose the desired thickness. To change the shading inside the box, open the Annotate menu, choose Shade, and choose the desired shading. To change the shape of the box's border or remove the border, open the Annotate menu, choose Border, and choose the desired border.

In addition to changing the look of the text box, you can change the look and alignment of the text inside the box as follows:

1. Click on the text box containing the text you want to format.

2. Click on the I-beam button, and then drag the mouse pointer over the text to be changed.

3. Perform one of the following steps:

 • To center or right-align the text, click on one of the text alignment buttons shown in Figure 12.2.

 • To make the text bold, italic, or underlined, click on the appropriate button.

- To change the type style, click on the down arrow to the right of the style box, and click on the desired font.

- To change the type size, click on the down arrow to the right of the type size box, and select the desired size in points. (There are 72 points in an inch.)

Using the Annotate Menu   Although the easiest way to change the look of the text is to use the formatting ribbon, you can also use the options listed on the **A**nnotate menu to change the look and alignment of the text.

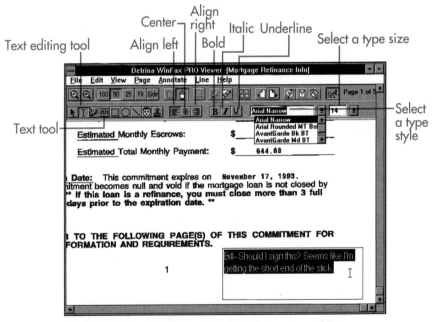

Figure 12.2   Use the tools on the formatting ribbon to change the look and layout of your text.

Adding Lines and Shapes

In addition to text, you can add lines, arrows, rectangles, and circles to a fax. Perform the following steps:

1. Click on the drawing tool you want to use:

 Pencil tool allows you to draw just as if you were using a pencil. You can draw a rough line or do curlicues.

 Box tool lets you draw squares and rectangles.

 Oval tool lets you draw circles and ovals.

 Line tool lets you draw straight lines and arrows.

2. Move the mouse pointer where you want one corner or end of the object to appear.

3. Hold down the mouse button, and drag the pointer to where you want the opposite corner or end of the object.

4. Release the mouse button. The object appears.

You can change the line thickness of any object before or after you draw it. If you already drew the object, select it. Open the Line menu, and choose the desired line thickness. The Line menu also contains options for drawing arrows.

With rectangles and ovals, you can also change the border shape and the shading inside the object. If you already drew the object, select it first. Then, open the Annotate menu, and select Border or Shade. Select the desired option.

Adding Graphic Files

If you have a clip art collection, or you created a picture using a paint or draw program, you can place the picture on a fax page. WinFax can handle the following graphic file formats:

Extension	Format
.BIN	Mac Paint
.BMP	Windows Bitmap
.EPS	Encapsulated Postscript
.FXS	WinFax
.GEM	GEM Line Art
.GIF	Graphic Interchange Format
.IMG	GEM Image
.PCX	PC Paintbrush
.TIF	Tagged Image File Format
.WMF	Windows Metafile

To place a graphic image on a fax page, perform the following steps:

1. Click on the graphic tool (the button with the guy's face).

2. Drag the mouse pointer to create a box where you want the picture placed. When you release the mouse button, the Graphics Attributes dialog box appears, prompting you to specify the name of the file you want to use.

3. Click on the Select button, and choose the drive, directory, and file name of the file.

4. Click on the OK button. WinFax returns you to the Graphics Attributes dialog box and inserts the file name of the selected file into the File Name text box.

5. Select one of the following Scaling options:

   None inserts the picture in its original size and dimensions, which may be too big or too small for the box you drew.

   Fit in Window makes the picture fit inside the box that WinFax places around it. This may distort the image.

   Aspect Fit keeps the relative dimensions of the picture the same, so the picture does not get distorted.

6. Click on the OK button. WinFax inserts the specified picture into the shaded box.

Changing Pictures If you decide later to use a different graphic file or change the scaling option you selected, double-click on the picture to display the Graphic Attributes dialog box, then enter your changes.

Selecting and Relayering Graphic Objects

To work with a line, shape, text box, or picture, you must first select it. The following list explains various ways to select objects:

- To select a single object, click on it.

- To select more than one object, hold down the Shift key while clicking on each object.

If one object is hidden behind the other, you must move the front object to the back in order to select the hidden object. To move an object to the top or bottom of a stack of objects, do this:

1. Click on any part of the object you want to move.

2. Open the Edit menu.

3. Select Bring to Front or Send to Back.

Quick Move   To quickly move an object to the back of a stack, select it, and press Ctrl+B. To move an object to the front, select it, and press Ctrl+T.

Cutting, Copying, and Pasting Objects

You can cut, copy, and paste selected objects by using the appropriate commands from the Edit menu. Perform the following steps:

1. Select the object(s) you want to copy or cut.

2. Open the Edit menu, and select Copy or Cut. The selected objects are placed on the Clipboard.

3. To paste the objects, open the Edit menu, and select Paste or press Ctrl+V. The objects are pasted from the Clipboard onto the page. You can move the objects as explained in the following section.

Moving and Resizing Graphics

Once you have placed a graphic object on the fax page, you can move it or resize it simply by dragging:

- To move an object, click on the object to select it, and then hold down the mouse button and drag the object to where you want it.

- To resize an object, click on the object to select it, and then drag one of the object's handles (the small squares that surround the object).

Preventing Distortion   To resize a graphic object while retaining the object's relative dimensions, drag the object's corner while holding down the Shift key.

Saving Your Annotations

The annotations you add to a fax page are saved on a separate layer that acts as an overlay transparency. You can save this transparency by itself or save it with the fax page to make the annotations a permanent part of the page. Save your annotations as follows:

1. Open the File menu.

2. Select one of the following Save options:

Save   To keep the annotations separate from the fax page.

Merge Annotation with Fax   To make the annotations part of the fax page.

   In this lesson, you learned how to annotate a fax page by adding text and pictures. In the next lesson, you will learn how to monitor a fax as it is being sent.

Lesson

Tracking Fax Send Progress

In this lesson, you will learn to monitor the progress of a fax being sent and how to cancel the fax.

Viewing Outgoing Fax Information

WinFax is set up to display the progress of a fax as it is being sent. To turn this display off or on, follow these steps:

1. Display the Delrina WinFax PRO main program window.

2. Open the Setup menu.

3. Select Program. The Program Setup dialog box appears, as shown in Figure 13.1.

4. Click on the Display Call Progress option to turn it on if it is off or off if it is on. (An **X** inside the check box indicates that the option is on.)

5. Click on the OK button.

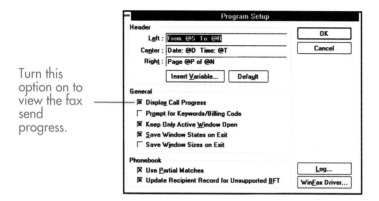

Turn this
option on to
view the fax
send
progress.

Figure 13.1   Turn on Display Call Progress to keep track of
the fax being sent.

With the Display Call Progress option on, WinFax
displays the Status dialog box, shown in Figure 13.2, as it
calls and transmits the fax. This dialog box displays the
following information:

Operation   Displays the status of the link between
your modem and the remote modem.

Identifier   Shows the recipient's CSID or station
identifier. This may be the fax number you called or
the company name.

Current Page   Shows how much of the current page
has been sent.

Destination   Shows the recipient's name as you
entered it.

Fax Number   Displays the recipient's fax number.

Page   Shows the number of the page currently being faxed and the total number of pages to fax.

Speed   Indicates the rate at which data is being transmitted from your modem to the remote modem.

> **No Status Dialog Box?**   If you turned the Display Call Progress option off, you can still view the call progress. Display the WinFax main program window. At the bottom of the window is a status bar that displays the progress of the call. Next to the call progress is an Abort button that you can use to cancel the call.

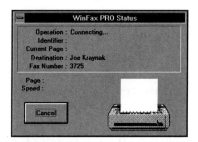

Figure 13.2   The Status dialog box displays the call progress.

Cancelling a Fax

There are two ways to cancel a fax as it is being transmitted. Either click on the Cancel button in the Status dialog box or click on the Abort button at the bottom of the WinFax main program window. WinFax immediately "hangs up" the fax modem and adds the fax to the Send Log as an unsuccessful attempt (a red X appears next to it).

Success or Failure?

WinFax is initially set to try sending a fax three times. If it is unsuccessful, the fax will appear in the Send Log with a red X next to it. If the Send Log is not displayed, you can display the log by performing the following steps:

1. Display the WinFax Pro program window.

2. Click on the Send Log button, or open the Send menu and choose Log. The Send Log appears, as shown in Figure 13.3.

> **Managing Sent Faxes**   For more details about using the Send and Receive Logs, see Lesson 24, "Managing Fax Events."

A check mark shows the fax was successfully transmitted.

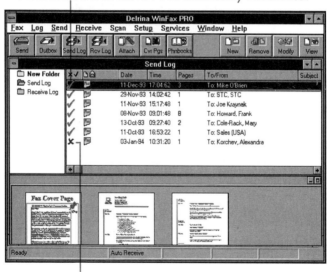

The X indicates an unsuccessful attempt.

Figure 13.3   The Send Log lists successful and unsuccessful attempts.

In this lesson, you learned how to monitor the transmission of a fax. In the next lesson, you will learn how to resend a fax that has not been transmitted successfully.

Lesson

Resending and Forwarding a Fax

In this lesson, you will learn how to resend a fax that you previously sent or received.

Resending a Fax

WinFax keeps a record of every fax you send (successfully or unsuccessfully) or receive in a fax log. To resend a fax you sent either successfully or unsuccessfully, take the following steps:

1. In the WinFax PRO main program window, click on the Send Log button, or open the Send menu and choose Log. WinFax displays a list of sent faxes, as in Figure 14.1.

Sent faxes   Send Log button

You can also double-click on the Send Log folder to view a list of sent faxes.

Figure 14.1 WinFax keeps a list of the faxes you send.

2. Select the fax you want to resend.

> **Unsure?** If you are not sure the fax you selected is the one you want to send, click on the View button to preview the fax.

3. Open the Log menu and select Resubmit. The Send dialog box appears with the name and fax number of the person to whom you originally sent the fax.

4. Change any of the options in the Send dialog box, as desired.

5. Click on the Send button.

6. Perform any other required steps to complete the fax transmission.

Forwarding a Received Fax

When you receive a fax, WinFax keeps a record of it in the Receive Log. You may want to annotate the fax (see Lessons 11 and 12) and send it back to the person who sent it, or you may want to forward the fax to another person. To forward a fax, perform the following steps:

1. In the WinFax Pro main program window, click on the Rcv Log button, or open the Receive menu and choose Log. WinFax displays a list of received faxes.

2. Click on the fax you want to forward.

3. Open the Log menu, and select Forward. The Forward dialog box appears, as shown in Figure 14.2.

The Forward dialog box displays three pages of the fax; to view more, use the scroll bar.

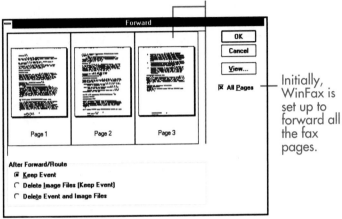

Initially, WinFax is set up to forward all the fax pages.

Figure 14.2   The Forward dialog box shows the fax pages that will be sent.

4. (Optional) To send only selected pages of the fax, click on the All Pages option to turn it off, and then click on the page you want to send. To send more than one page, hold down the Shift key while clicking on each page.

5. (Optional) To preview the fax or add text or graphics to the fax page(s), click on the View button. (For details, see Lessons 11 and 12.)

6. Click on the OK button. The Send dialog box appears.

7. Type the name of the person to whom you are faxing this document.

8. Press the Tab key, or click inside the Number text box, and type the recipient's fax number.

9. (Optional) Change any desired options in the Send dialog box.

10. Click on the Send button.

11. Perform any other required steps to complete the fax transmission.

> **Autoforwarding Faxes** If you are away from your computer, you can have WinFax forward the faxes to a fax machine (or another computer that has a fax modem). See Lesson 19 for details.

In this lesson, you learned how to resend a fax you already sent and how to forward a fax you have received. In the next two lessons, you will learn how to work with phonebooks.

Lesson

Making and Selecting Your Own Phonebook

In this lesson, you will learn how to create and select a phonebook for organizing your phone numbers.

Creating a Phonebook

WinFax contains a default phonebook (see Lesson 4) that you can use to store the names and fax numbers of the people to whom you fax. This phonebook may be sufficient for your needs. However, if you need to keep separate phonebooks (for instance, one for personal numbers and one for customers), you can create additional phonebooks. Here's how:

1. Display the WinFax PRO main program window.

2. Open the Fax menu, and select Phonebooks, or click on the Phnbooks button. The Phonebook window appears.

3. Double-click on the New Phonebook/Group icon shown in Figure 15.1. The Add Phonebook/Group dialog box appears as shown.

Double-click on this icon to display the
Add Phonebook/Group dialog box.

Type a name for
the phonebook.

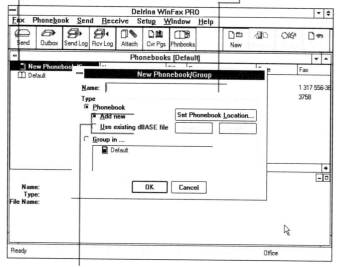

Make sure these options are selected.

Figure 15.1   You must name your new phonebook.

4. Type a name for the phonebook (40 characters or
   fewer) in the Name text box.

5. Make sure the Phonebook and Add new options are
   selected.

> **The Group in Option**   Don't worry about the
> **G**roup in option. This option allows you to group
> recipients in a phonebook, so you can send the
> same fax to all the recipients. See Lesson 16 for
> details.

6. Click on the OK button.

WinFax creates the phonebook file, and stores the file in the \WINFAX\DATA directory. The name that WinFax gives the file is based on the first seven characters of the name you typed in step 4. If you ever create a phonebook and want to store it in a different directory, or assign it a different file name, use the Set Program Location button in the Add Phonebook/Group dialog box.

Selecting a Phonebook

You can select a phonebook in the Send dialog box. Pull down the Phonebooks list, as shown in Figure 15.2, and then click on the phonebook you want to use.

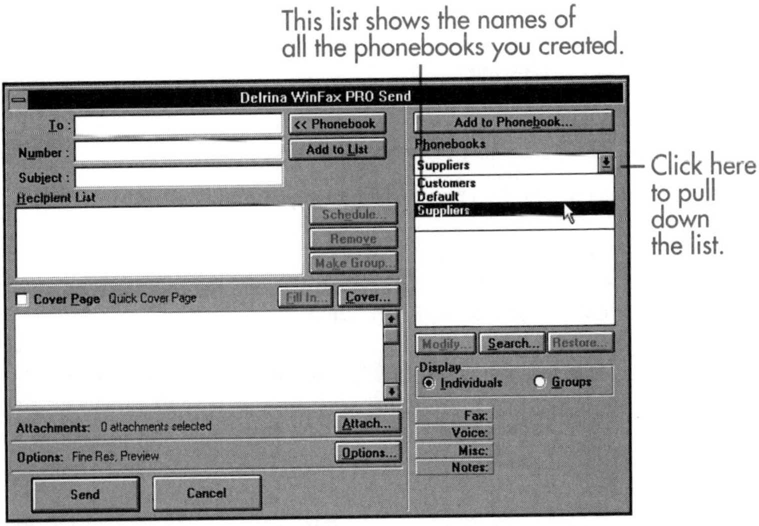

Figure 15.2 You can select a phonebook in the Send Fax dialog box.

If you want to use a specific phonebook as the default (so you don't have to select it each time you send a fax), do the following:

1. Display the WinFax PRO main program window.

2. If the Phonebook list is not displayed, open the Fax menu and select Phonebooks, or click on the Phnbooks button.

3. In the Phonebook list, double-click on the phonebook you want to use as the default. The Phonebook icon changes to an open book, indicating that this phonebook is now the default.

Adding Names and Fax Numbers

You can add names and fax numbers to your new phonebook the same way you add names and numbers to the WinFax default phonebook. For complete instructions, refer to Lesson 4.

You can also add phonebook entries to a phonebook by copying or moving the entries from one phonebook to another, as follows:

1. If the Phonebook list is not displayed, open the Fax menu, and select Phonebooks, or click on the Phnbooks button.

2. Double-click on the phonebook that contains the phonebook entries you want to copy or move.

3. Hold down the Ctrl key, and click on each entry you want to copy or move. (You can select several neighboring entries by holding down the Shift key while clicking on the first and last entry in the group.)

4. Move the mouse pointer over one of the selected entries.

5. Hold down the mouse button (and the Ctrl button, if you want to copy the entries), and drag the mouse pointer over the phonebook icon in which you want to add the entries.

6. Release the mouse button. If you held down the Ctrl key while dragging, WinFax copies the entries to the group. If you did not hold down the Ctrl key, WinFax moves the entries.

Removing a Phonebook

You can delete a phonebook you no longer use. However, first make sure it does not contain any phone numbers that you may need again. (If a phonebook contains entries you will need, you can copy or move the entries to another phonebook, as explained in the previous section.) If you are certain you want to delete a phonebook, perform the following steps:

1. Display the WinFax PRO main program window.

2. If the Phonebook list is not displayed, open the Fax menu, and select Phonebooks, or click on the Phnbooks button.

3. In the phonebook list, click on the phonebook you want to delete.

4. Click on the Remove button, or open the Phonebook menu and select Remove. A dialog box appears, asking you to confirm the deletion.

5. To delete the phonebook, select Yes. To keep the phonebook, click on No.

In this lesson, you learned how to create, select, and delete phonebooks. In the next lesson, you will learn how to perform more advanced tasks, such as creating recipient groups, sorting the recipients in a phonebook, and merging two phonebooks.

Lesson

16

Advanced Phonebook Features

In this lesson, you will learn how to use advanced phonebook features, such as creating recipient groups, sorting the recipients in a phonebook, and searching the phonebook list.

Creating Recipient Groups

If you frequently send the same faxes to two or more people, you may want to create a group that includes those people. Then, when you send a fax to the group, a copy goes to every member. The easiest way to create a *recipient group* is to use the Send dialog box as follows:

1. Display the Delrina WinFax PRO Send dialog box.

2. Add to the Recipient List the names of the people you want to group. (You can select names from a phonebook or type a name and number and click on the Add to List button.)

Drag and Drop   To quickly add recipients from the phonebook list to the Recipient List, drag the names in the phonebook list to the Recipient List area.

3. In the Recipient List, select the names to include in the group. (Either hold down the Ctrl key while clicking on each name, or hold down the Shift key while clicking on the first and last names in the list.)

4. Click on the Make Group button. The Make Group dialog box appears, as shown in Figure 16.1.

5. Type a name for the group (40 characters or fewer) in the Name text box.

6. From the Group in list, click on the phonebook in which you want the group added.

7. Click on the OK button. The group is added to the specified phonebook.

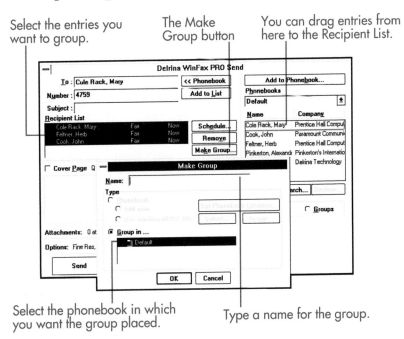

Select the entries you want to group.

The Make Group button

You can drag entries from here to the Recipient List.

Select the phonebook in which you want the group placed.

Type a name for the group.

Figure 16.1 The Add Group dialog box lets you create a group of recipients.

To send a fax to a group, perform the following steps:

1. Display the Delrina WinFax PRO Send dialog box.

2. Click on the Groups option, shown in Figure 16.2. WinFax displays a list of the groups you created.

3. Click on the Add to List button. The group name is added to the Recipient List.

4. (Optional) Add any other names to the Recipient List.

5. Perform any other steps required to send the fax (See Lessons 2 and 3), and then click on the Send button.

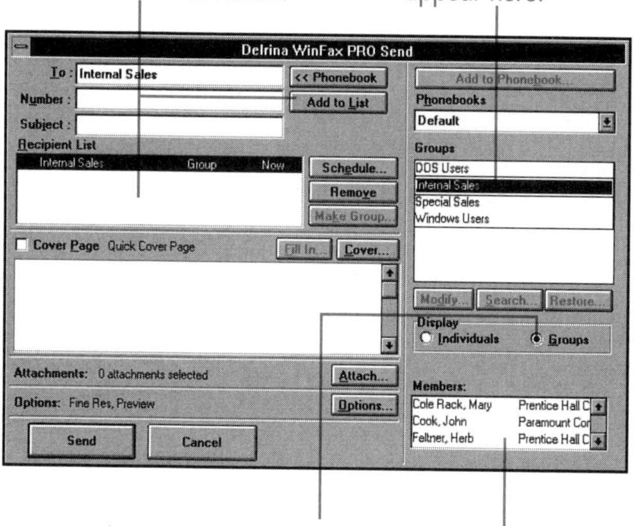

Select a group, and then click on the Add to List button.

The groups you created appear here.

Select Groups to display a list of groups.

The members in the selected group appear here.

Figure 16.2 Select Groups to display the Group(s) you created.

Viewing the List of Individuals   WinFax can display either individual or group names, but not both. To switch back to a listing of individuals, click on the Individuals option.

Grouping in the Phonebook Window

Although the Send dialog box provides the most convenient way to group phonebook entries, you can also group in the Phonebook window. Perform the following steps to create a recipient group in the Phonebook window:

1. Display the WinFax PRO main program window.

2. If the Phonebook list is not displayed, open the Fax menu, and select Phonebooks, or click on the Phnbooks button.

3. Click on the phonebook icon for the phonebook in which you want to create the group.

4. Open the Phonebook menu, and select New. The New Phonebook/Group dialog box appears.

5. Type a name for the group (40 characters or fewer) in the Name text box.

6. Select the Group in option.

7. From the Group in list, click on the phonebook in which you want the group added.

8. Click on the OK button. The Group is added to the specified phonebook.

Whenever a phonebook contains one or more groups, its icon (in the Phonebook window) appears with a + or - to the left of it. The + indicates that the phonebook contains groups that are not displayed. (The minus means all groups are displayed.) You can display the groups as follows:

1. Click on the phonebook icon whose groups you want to view.

2. Open the Phonebook menu, and select Expand Folder. Group icons appear below the phonebook icon, and the plus sign (+) changes to a minus sign (-).

3. To hide the groups, open the Phonebook menu, and select Collapse Folder.

> **Quick with a Click** You can quickly expand a phonebook folder by clicking on the plus sign to the left of the phonebook's icon. To collapse an expanded folder, click on the minus sign.

Once you have created a group, you can drag phonebook entries onto the group's icon, as follows:

1. Double-click on the phonebook that contains the entries you want to add to a group. (You can add entries from any phonebook.)

2. Hold down the Ctrl key, and click on each entry you want to add to the group. (You can select several neighboring entries by holding down the Shift key while clicking on the first and last entry in the group.)

3. Move the mouse pointer over one of the selected entries.

4. Hold down the mouse button, and drag the mouse pointer over the group icon to which you want to add the entries, as in Figure 16.3. (To copy, rather than move, the entries, hold down the Ctrl key while dragging.)

5. Release the mouse button. WinFax copies the entries to the group.

Drag selected individuals to the group
in which you want them placed.

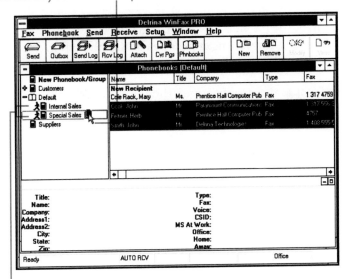

Groups

Figure 16.3 Drag the selected entries over the group icon.

Sorting Your Phonebook Entries

The phonebook entries in the Send Fax dialog box are
initially sorted in alphabetical order (A–Z) by last name. To
sort the entries by company name instead, click on the
Company option in the Send dialog box Phonebook panel
(see Figure 16.2). WinFax resorts the entries by company
name from A to Z.

> **Sorting in the Phonebook Window** You
> can sort phonebook entries in the Phonebook
> window as well. Display the Phonebook window
> (Fax/Phonebooks), double-click on the phonebook
> whose entries you want to sort, and then open the
> Phonebook menu, and select Sort by Name or Sort by
> Company.

Searching for a Phonebook Entry

If you have a phonebook with many entries, it may be ineffi-
cient to look for a specific entry by scrolling through the list.
To find an entry more quickly, search for it as follows:

1. In the Send dialog box, click on the Search button
   (just below the phone number list). The Search
   dialog box appears. Figure 16.4 shows a Search
   dialog box with a sample entry.

2. Type an entry in each text box you want to use for
   the search. For example, you can type Elizabeth in
   the First Name text box to find the phone book
   entries for everyone named Elizabeth. You can type
   E in the First Name text box and S in the Last text
   box to find entries for all those whose first name
   starts with E and whose last name starts with S.

3. Click on the OK button. You return to the Send
   dialog box, and the list displays all entries that
   match your search instructions.

Viewing the Complete List   To view the complete
list of phonebook entries, click on the Restore
button, just below the list of entries. If that doesn't
work, repeat the search, and clear all your search
entries.

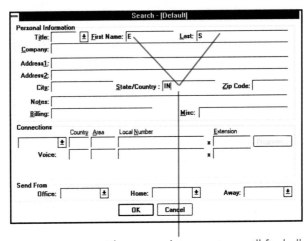

These search instructions will find all entries with a first name starting with E, a last name starting with S, and a state listed as IN.

Figure 16.4 Type entries to tell WinFax what to search for.

In this lesson, you learned how to create recipient groups, sort phonebook entries, and search for specific entries. In the next lesson, you will learn how to control the information that is placed on the cover pages.

Lesson 17

Editing the Cover Page Contents

In this lesson, you will learn how to change the information that appears on the cover page.

What Does WinFax Put on Fax Pages?

Whenever you send a fax, WinFax inserts information at the top of each fax page in a *header*. By default, the header includes your name, the date and time, the total number of fax pages, and the current fax page. In addition, some cover pages include a section at the bottom that contains the recipient's name; your name, voice number, and fax number; and the total number of pages in the fax.

> **What's a Header?** A header is any information that is printed at the top of every page.

In this lesson, you will learn how to specify which data you want printed in the header and on the cover page.

Changing Your User Information

When you installed WinFax, the installation program prompted you to enter your name, fax number, and phone number. Whenever you send a fax, this information is placed on the cover page and in the header. To change the information, take the following steps:

1. Change to the WinFax PRO program window, if necessary.

2. Open the Setup menu, and choose User. The User Setup dialog box appears, as shown in Figure 17.1.

3. Type your name, company's name, fax number, and phone number in the appropriate text boxes. (Use the mouse, or Tab key, to move from text box to text box.)

4. Click on the OK button, or press Enter. You are returned to the WinFax PRO program window.

WinFax inserts this information in the header and cover page.

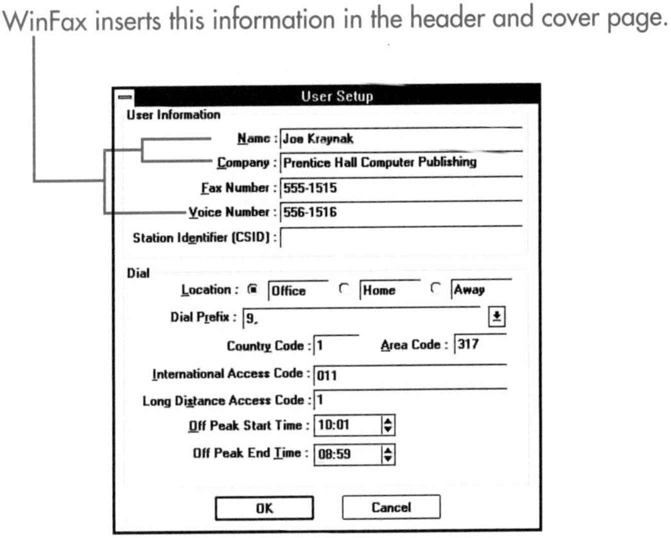

Figure 17.1 The User Setup dialog box lets you enter information about yourself.

Changing the Fax Header

The header that appears on the top of each fax page uses codes that pull your name and fax number from the User Setup fields and take the date and time from your computer. You can change the codes to insert different information or to reposition the information on the fax pages by performing the following steps:

1. Open the Setup menu, and select Program. The Program Setup dialog box appears, as shown in Figure 17.2. (The @ codes insert specific information in the header; for example, @D inserts the date.)

2. To change any text (such as From:) click inside the text box with the entry to be changed, and then edit the text as usual.

3. To delete an @ code, delete both the @ sign and the letter that follows it.

4. To insert an @ code, click where you want the code placed, click on the Insert Variable button, and then click on the code you want to insert.

5. When you are done modifying the information, click on the OK button.

Mess Up the Header?   If you edit the header information and decide later that you prefer WinFax's original header, display the Program Setup dialog box and click on the Default button.

Header text and codes   To return to the original header, click on this button.

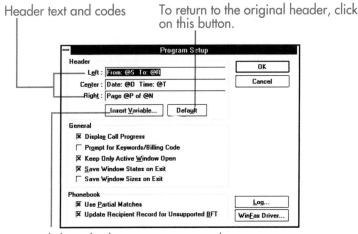

Click on this button to insert a code.

Figure 17.2 Edit the header information to control the content and position of it.

Changing Cover Page Variables

Like the header, the cover page contains variables that insert information about you, the recipient, the time and date, and the number of fax pages. To change this information, you must open the cover page in the Cover Page Designer, and cut and paste the required codes, as follows:

1. Display the Delrina WinFax PRO main program window.

2. Click on the Cvr Pgs button in the button bar, or open the Fax menu and select Cover Pages. The Cover Pages window appears, showing several groups of cover pages.

3. Double-click on the file (on the left side of the window) that you think has the cover page you want to edit. Each file in the list contains several

cover pages. The Description list displays the names of the cover pages.

4. From the Description list, click on the cover page you want. A sketch of the cover page appears at the bottom of the window.

5. When you have selected the cover page you want to edit, click on the View button, or open the Fax menu and select View. The cover page is opened in the Cover Page Designer.

6. Use the scroll bar, as shown in Figure 17.3, to move down to the area that contains the variables you want to change.

7. Click on the box that contains the variables you want to change. Handles (small boxes) appear around the box to indicate that it has been selected.

8. Click on the I-beam button in the button bar, and then click inside the text box where you want to edit the text.

9. Edit any text as you normally would.

10. (Optional) To delete a code, drag the mouse pointer over the code, and press Del.

11. (Optional) To insert a code, click where you want the code inserted, and then open the Variable menu, and select the code.

12. (Optional) To edit an entry in another text box, click inside the text box, and repeat steps 9-11.

13. To save your changes, open the File menu, and select Save.

Saving a Copy   To keep the original cover page and create a new cover page with your changes, open the File menu, and select Save As. Type a name for the copy, and then click on the OK button.

14. To exit the Cover Page Designer, open the File menu, and select Exit.

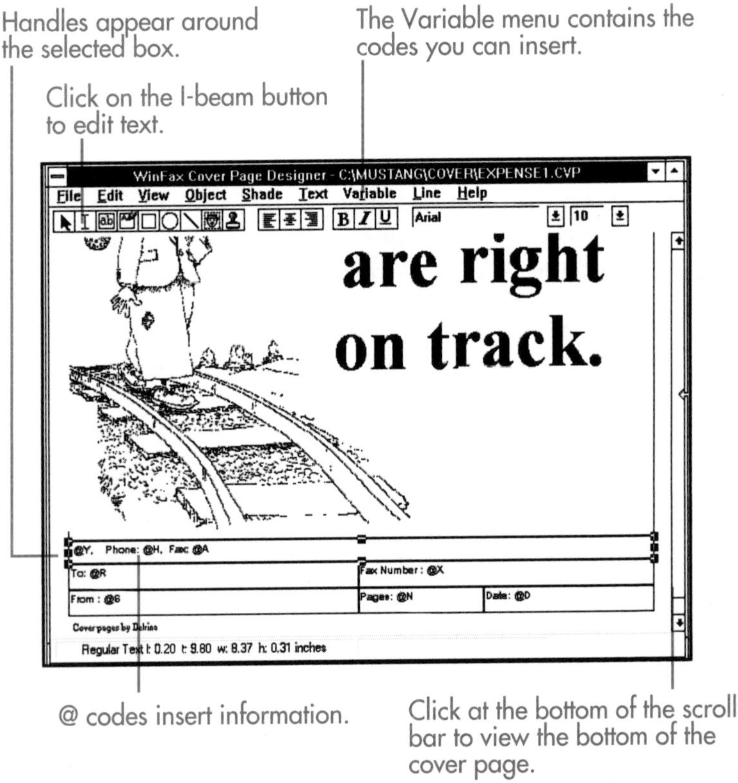

Handles appear around the selected box.

The Variable menu contains the codes you can insert.

Click on the I-beam button to edit text.

@ codes insert information.

Click at the bottom of the scroll bar to view the bottom of the cover page.

Figure 17.3   Most cover pages have codes that you can change.

In this lesson, you learned how to change the information that appears on the cover page and at the top of each fax page. In the next lesson, you will learn how to change the look of a cover page and create your own cover page.

Lesson

Making and Changing Cover Pages

In this lesson, you will learn how to create your own cover page and how to alter an existing cover page.

Making a New Cover Page

You can make a cover page from scratch or by modifying an existing cover page. The following steps cover both options:

1. Display the Delrina WinFax PRO main program window.

2. If the Cover Pages window is not displayed, click on the Cvr Pgs button, or open the Fax menu, and select Cover Pages. (See Figure 18.1.)

3. Double-click on the folder (on the left side of the window) to which you want the new cover page added.

> **Create Your Own Folder** To create your own folder, double-click on New Folder at the top of the list. Type a name for the folder, and then click on the OK button. Double-click on the folder to open it.

Each folder contains a group of related cover pages.

Click on this button to view a list of cover pages.

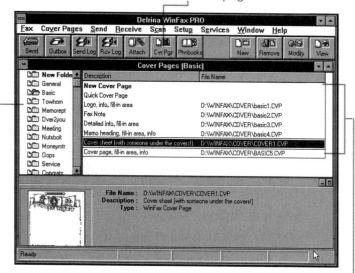

Individual cover pages are listed here.

Figure 18.1 The Cover Pages window displays groups of cover pages.

4. In the Description list, double-click on New Cover Page, or click on it and then click on the New button in the button bar. The New Cover Page dialog box appears.

5. Perform one of the following steps:

   • To create a cover page from scratch, click on the Design button. This starts the Cover Page Designer, displaying a blank cover page.

   • To modify an existing cover page, click on the Select button, choose the cover page you want to use, and click on the OK button. Then, click on the Design button. This opens the selected cover page in the Cover Page Designer, as shown in Figure 18.2.

6. Use the tools as described later in this lesson, to create or modify the cover page.

> **Changing the Cover Page View**   You can change the display size of the cover page to zoom in or out as you work. For example, you may want to zoom out to place and rearrange objects on the page, and zoom in to type text. To zoom in or out, select the desired size from the **V**iew menu.

7. After you have added one or two objects to the page, perform one of the following steps:

   • If you are creating the cover page by modifying an existing cover page, open the File menu, and select Save As.

   • If you are creating the cover page from scratch, open the File menu, and select Save.

8. Type a file name (up to eight characters), and click on the OK button. WinFax adds the extension CVP to the file name and saves the file in the \WINFAX\COVER directory.

> **Save Regularly**   As you design your cover page, be sure to enter the File Save command (or press Ctrl+S) every 5 or 10 minutes to avoid losing your work.

9. After creating your cover page, open the File menu, and select Exit. You are returned to the New Cover Page dialog box.

10. Type a description of the cover page (up to 59 characters) in the **D**escription text box.

11. Click on the OK button. The new cover page appears in the list of cover pages.

Tool for selecting objects   Tools for creating objects

Tool for selecting text   Text styling tools

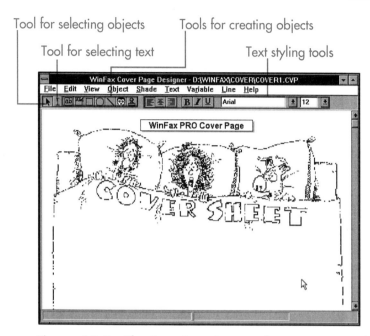

Figure 18.2   The Cover Page Designer lets you create and modify cover pages.

Adding Text Boxes and Shapes to a Cover Page

Just below the menu bar is a button bar that contains several tools for placing text, pictures, and shapes on a page. To place a text box or shape (rectangle, oval, or line) on a page, perform the following steps:

1. Click on the tool you want to use:

 Regular text tool lets you add text that will become a permanent part of the cover page.

 Fillable text tool inserts a text box that you can type in later (when you choose to send the fax).

☐ Box tool lets you draw squares and rectangles.

◎ Oval tool lets you draw circles and ovals.

◢ Line tool lets you draw straight lines and arrows.

2. Move the mouse pointer where you want one corner or end of the object to appear.

3. Hold down the mouse button, and drag the pointer to where you want the opposite corner or end of the object.

4. Release the mouse button. The object appears.

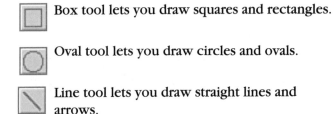

Adding Predrawn Pictures   You can add clip art or pictures you have drawn or scanned to a cover page by clicking on the Graphic tool (the button with the guy's face on it), and then clicking where you want the picture placed. For details, refer to "Adding Graphic Files" in Lesson 12.

Changing the Look of an Object

The objects you place on a cover page work in much the same way as objects you would use to annotate a fax in the WinFax Viewer. For details on how to select, cut, copy, paste, move, and format objects, refer to Lesson 12. The following list provides a review of what you can do:

- **Select an object**   Click on the object. To select more than one object, hold down the Ctrl key while clicking on each object.

- **Relayer objects**   If an object is in front of or behind another object, you can relayer the objects to achieve the desired look. Click on the object you want to move, open the Object menu, and select Bring to Front or Send to **Back**.

- **Change the line thickness**   Select the object, open the Line menu, and select the desired line thickness.

- **Change the border shape**   Select the object whose border shape you want to change, open the Object menu, select Border, and select the desired border.

- **Change the shading within the border**   Select the object whose shading you want to change, open the Shade menu, and select the desired shading.

- **Change the look of text**   Click on the Text Editing button (the button with the I-beam on it), drag the mouse pointer over the text you want to change, and click on the desired text tool in the ribbon. (You can also change the look of the text by selecting the desired text size, style, and alignment from the **Text** menu.)

- **Cut, Copy, and Paste Objects**   Select the object(s) you want to cut or copy, open the Edit menu, and select Copy or Cut. To paste the objects, open the Edit menu, and select Paste.

- **Move an Object**   Select the object(s) you want to move. Move the mouse pointer over any of the selected object(s), hold down the mouse button, and drag the object(s) to the desired position. Release the mouse button.

- **Resize an Object**   Select the object you want to resize. Drag one of the object's handles (the small squares that surround the object).

Preventing Distortion   To resize an object while retaining the object's relative dimensions, hold down the Shift key while dragging the object's corner.

In this lesson, you learned how to create and modify cover pages. The next part of this book contains lessons that explain how to receive faxes and work with faxes you have received.

Receiving Faxes in Windows

In this lesson, you will learn several options for receiving faxes in Windows automatically and manually.

Turning Automatic Reception On or Off

When you first start WinFax, it is not set up to receive faxes. To receive a fax, you must turn on automatic reception or choose to receive a fax manually.

> **Automatic or Manual Reception?** If you have a separate phone line for your modem, you can turn on automatic reception so that WinFax will receive faxes in the background while you work in your other Windows programs. If you have one phone line that you use for both voice and fax calls, you should manually receive faxes, as explained later in this lesson.

To turn automatic reception on or off:

1. Make sure your fax modem is on.

2. Run WinFax PRO, as explained in Lesson 1.

3. Open the Receive menu.

4. Select Automatic Receive. The status bar (at the
   bottom of the window) displays **Auto Receive:
   Enabled** or **Auto Receive: Disabled** to indicate
   the current setting.

5. (Optional) Click on the Minimize button in the
   upper right corner of the program window to get
   it out of the way. WinFax remains running but is
   reduced to an icon.

> **WinFax Must Be Running**   In order to
> receive incoming faxes, your fax modem must be
> on, and your computer must be running Win-
> dows and WinFax PRO.

Whenever WinFax receives a fax, it notifies you and
adds the fax to the Receive Log. To view or print a fax, refer
to Lesson 20.

Setting the Receive Options

WinFax is set initially to answer incoming calls on the first
ring and notify you of any incoming faxes. To view a fax as it
arrives, print it after it is received, or choose other options,
take these steps:

1. Open the Setup menu, and select Receive. The
   Receive Setup dialog box appears, as shown in
   Figure 19.1.

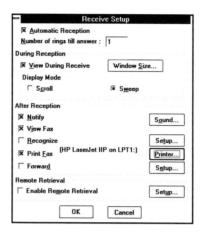

Figure 19.1 You can tell WinFax how to handle incoming faxes.

2. Turn automatic reception on or off by clicking on the Automatic Reception option. An **X** inside the check box indicates that Auto Reception is on.

3. Click inside the Number of rings till answer text box, and type the number of times you want the fax modem to "ring" before WinFax answers it.

4. To look at the fax pages as they come in, click on the View During Receive option.

Changing the Window Size   You can change the size of the window in which WinFax displays the incoming fax by clicking on the Window Size button. A sample window appears. Drag its borders to change the size and shape of the window, and then double-click on the Control-menu button or press Alt+F4.

5. In the Display mode section, select one of these options:

Scroll displays the fax pages inching up from the bottom of the window.

Sweep displays the fax pages being displayed from the top to the bottom of the window.

6. To tell WinFax what to do after receiving the fax, select one or more of the following After Reception options:

Notify tells WinFax to sound a beep and display a dialog box whenever a fax is received. You can click on the Sound button, and choose a sound file (with the **.WAV** extension) to have WinFax emit a sound of your choice.

View Fax displays the received fax in the WinFax Viewer. To learn more about the Viewer, see Lesson 20.

Recognize turns optical character recognition (OCR) on. This transforms an incoming fax into editable text. For details, refer to Lesson 21.

Print Fax tells WinFax to send the fax to your computer's printer to give you a printed copy of the fax. Use the Printer button to specify the printer you want to use.

Forward tells WinFax to dial the number of another fax machine (or another computer that is running a fax application), and send the fax to that machine.

Automatically Forwarding Faxes   If you turned on the Forward option, click on the Setup button to enter the fax number to which you want received faxes forwarded. The dialog box that appears allows you to enter other preferences, as well.

7. (Optional) To be able to retrieve received faxes when you are away from your office, click on Enable Remote Retrieval. (You can then use the **Receive/Retrieve** Remote option to call into your office computer and get your faxes.)

8. Click on the OK button.

Receiving Faxes Manually

If you have one phone line for both voice and fax calls, you don't want WinFax answering all your calls. To receive a fax, you must know approximately when it is coming, and then choose the Manual Receive option:

1. Wait until you hear your fax modem "ringing."

2. Open the Receive menu, and select Manual Receive Now. WinFax answers the call and receives the fax.

Running DOS Programs from Windows   If you run a DOS program from Windows, be sure to run the program inside a window in Windows. Otherwise, you will not be able to receive a fax while working in the DOS program.

In this lesson, you learned how to use WinFax to receive faxes manually and how to set up WinFax to receive faxes automatically.

Lesson

20

Viewing, Printing, and Cleaning Up a Fax

In this lesson, you will learn how to view and print a received fax and how to clean up a fax that may have suffered from line noise.

Viewing and Printing Faxes

If you turned on the View Fax and Print Fax options in the Receive Setup dialog box (see Lesson 19), incoming faxes are automatically printed and displayed in the WinFax Viewer. If the View Fax and Print Fax options are off, you can view and print a fax as follows:

1. Display the Delrina WinFax PRO main program window.

2. Click on the Rcv Log button, or open the Receive menu and select Log. A list of received faxes appears.

3. Click on the fax you want to view or print.

4. Click on the View button, or open the Fax menu and select View. The fax appears in the Viewer. (For help with Viewer, see Lesson 11.)

5. To print the fax, open the File menu, and select Print. The Print Fax dialog box appears, as shown in Figure 20.1.

6. Select one of the following options to specify which pages you want to print:

All to print all the fax pages.

From ___ **to** ___ to print a range of pages. Type entries in the two text boxes to specify the range of pages you want to print.

7. To specify a different printer, click on the Printer button, click on the desired printer, and click on OK.

8. (Optional) To print 4 tiny fax pages per paper page, click on the 4 Faxes/Page option.

9. Click on the OK button to start printing.

Select All to print all of the fax pages.   Make sure you don't have WinFax as your printer.

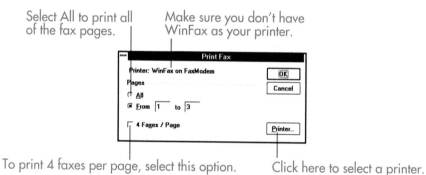

To print 4 faxes per page, select this option.   Click here to select a printer.

Figure 20.1   Use the Print Page(s) dialog box to print the displayed fax pages.

Print without Viewing   You can print a fax from the Send Log or Receive Log without display-ing it in the viewer. Simply select the fax you want to print, open the **Fax** menu, and select Print Event.

Cleaning Up the Line Noise Dots

When a fax machine sends a digital representation of a page over the phone lines, the page may pick up dots and shading from line noise. Before printing or forwarding a fax, you can remove these dots to make it more readable and improve its appearance. Follow these steps:

1. Display the fax you want to clean up in the Viewer, as explained earlier in this lesson.

2. Open the Edit menu, and select Cleanup. The Cleanup Fax dialog box appears, as shown in Figure 20.2.

3. Under **Area** select one of the following options:

   Entire Page to clean the entire fax page that is displayed.

   Visible Portion to clean only the part displayed in the Viewer.

> **Cleaning Up a Selected Area** The Selected Area option in Figure 20.2 is not available because no area was selected. To clean an area, select the area before selecting the **C**leanup option from the **E**dit menu.

4. In the **Degree** section choose how heavy the cleaning will be. The more dots removed, the lighter your fax page becomes. Light removes a few extraneous dots; Medium removes more; and Heavy removes the most dots.

5. Click on the OK button. A dialog box appears, showing you the progress of the cleaning.

Undoing a Cleanup You can undo a cleanup but only immediately after entering the command. Open the Edit menu, and select Undo.

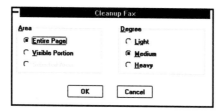

Figure 20.2   Use the Cleanup Fax dialog box to specify an area and degree of cleanup.

Saving a Cleaned Fax

After you clean a fax, save the fax file to protect your changes:

1. Open the File menu.

2. Select Save. WinFax saves the file to disk.

In this lesson, you learned how to view, print, and clean up a fax you received. In the next lesson, you will learn how to use WinFax's OCR (optical character recognition) feature to transform a fax into editable text.

Lesson

21

Turning a Fax into Editable Text

In this lesson, you will learn how to use WinFax's optical character recognition feature to transform a fax you received into a text file that you can open and edit in your word processing program.

What Is Optical Character Recognition?

WinFax comes with an optical character recognition (OCR) feature that can transform text on fax pages you received into text that you can edit in a word processing program. OCR compares the graphic version of each character (on the fax pages) to standard character shapes. OCR then transforms the graphic characters into standard text.

You can choose to have WinFax save the text in a file, open the file in your word processing program, display the text on-screen, or place the text on the Windows Clipboard. In any case, you can then edit the text in your word processing program.

Memory Requirements for Using OCR

To use the OCR feature, your computer must have at least eight megabytes of available memory. This can include RAM memory and Windows memory (a portion of disk storage that Windows treats as RAM).

Memory Requirements   To see how much memory is available, open the Help menu in Program Manager, and select the About command. To use disk space as virtual memory in Windows, refer to your Windows documentation.

Setting Up to Recognize Text

The most critical part of transforming fax text into editable text is in setting up to do it. This is the point at which you tell WinFax how you want the text handled during and after the character recognition process. To set up, perform the following steps:

1. Run the WinFax Viewer. You can run the Viewer by double-clicking on its icon in the WinFax PRO program group window or by selecting a received fax in the Receive Log and clicking on the View button.

2. If no fax file is open, use the File Open command to open the fax file whose text you want to recognize.

3. Open the Recognize menu, and select Setup. The Recognition Setup dialog box appears. Figure 21.1 shows a sample of a completed dialog box.

4. In the Areas on the Page section, choose one of the following options:

   Manually Select Areas if you want to recognize text on only selected portions of the fax page. This is useful if the fax page contains graphics.

   Auto Recognize if you want to recognize text on the entire fax page.

5. In the Options area, select the desired language from the Language list, and type the desired reject character in the Reject Character text box.

Choose this option to recognize text on entire pages.   Choose this option to recognize only selected text.

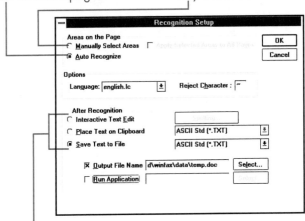

Select an option to tell WinFax what to do with the text.

Figure 21.1 Use the Recognition Setup dialog box to enter your preferences.

Reject Character The WinFax inserts the reject character whenever WinFax fails to recognize a character.

6. In the After Recognition area, select any of the following options:

Interactive Text Edit displays the text on-screen immediately after WinFax transforms it into editable text. You can then edit the text and save it.

Place Text on Clipboard copies the transformed text to the Windows Clipboard. You can use the Paste command in your favorite word processor to put the text in a document.

Save Text to File saves the text to a file on your computer's hard disk. You can then open the file and edit it.

7. If you chose **P**lace Text on Clipboard or **S**ave Text to File, open the drop-down list to the right of the option, and select the desired format for the text. ASCII Std (*.TXT) is a safe choice.

8. If you chose Save Text to File, choose one or both of the following options:

   Output File Name to give the file a name and specify the drive and directory on which to store the file. Type a drive, directory, and file name for the file in the text box.

   Run Application tells WinFax to run your word processing program and open the text file so you can edit it. In the text box to the right of the option, type the drive, directory, and file name of the file that runs the program.

9. Click on the OK button. The Recognition Setup dialog box disappears, and your setup settings are saved.

   Once you have set up the character recognition feature, you can recognize selected text or entire pages of text. If your fax pages contain only text (no graphics, logos, or lines), go to the next section to learn how to recognize entire pages of text. If your fax contains both text and graphics (or if you want to recognize only select portions of text), skip ahead to "Recognizing Selected Text."

Recognizing Entire Pages of Text

You can direct WinFax to recognize entire pages of text as follows:

1. In the WinFax Viewer, display the fax whose text you want to recognize.

2. Display the Recognition Setup dialog box (see previous section) and turn on Auto Recognize. Click on the OK button.

3. Perform one of the following steps:

To recognize a single page, use the Next Page or Previous Page button to display the page. Open the Recognize menu, and select Current Page.

To recognize a range of pages, open the Recognize menu, and choose Select Pages. Select All, or select From ___ to ___, and type a range of pages in the text boxes. Click on the OK button.

A dialog box appears, displaying the OCR progress. If you chose to save the text in a file or place it on the Windows Clipboard, the text is placed where you specified. If you chose Interactive Text Edit, the text appears in a separate window at the bottom of the screen. Edit the text, and then open the File menu, and select Save to save the text in a file.

OCR Is Not 100% Reliable   Be sure you read, edit, and spell-check the resulting text. Although OCR technology has improved over the years, it is still not 100% accurate.

Recognizing Selected Text

If you have a fax page that contains graphics or dark areas, you can direct WinFax to recognize only selected portions of text as follows:

1. In the WinFax Viewer, display the fax whose text you want to recognize.

2. Display the Recognition Setup dialog box, as explained in the previous section, and turn on the Manually Select Areas option.

3. Click on the OK button.

Selecting Areas on More Than One Page Normally, when you select an area on a page, the selected area applies only to that page. However, you can select Apply Selected Areas to All Pages to have the selected area on one page select the same areas on specified pages.

4. Perform one of the following steps:

To recognize a single page, use the Next Page or Previous Page button to display the page. Open the Recognize menu, and select Current Page.

To recognize a range of pages, open the Recognize menu, and choose Select Pages. Select All, or select From ___ to ___, and type a range of pages in the text boxes. Click on the OK button.

No matter which step you perform, the fax appears, as shown in Figure 21.2, with a toolbar that allows you to select the areas of text you want to recognize.

5. Click on the Draw Zones tool to enable the mouse pointer to select text.

6. Move the mouse pointer to the upper left corner of the area you want to recognize.

7. Hold down the mouse button, and drag the pointer to the lower right corner of the area you want to recognize.

8. Release the mouse button. A box appears around the selected area.

9. Repeat steps 5–8 to mark additional areas. Notice that as you mark areas, a number appears in the upper left corner of each marked area. These numbers represent the order in which the areas will be recognized.

Working with the Selected Area Boxes You can change the position and size of the box you drew around an area by clicking on the mouse pointer button in the toolbar and clicking on the box. Handles (small black boxes) appear around the box. Drag a handle to change the size or dimensions of the box. To move the box, move the mouse pointer anywhere inside it, hold down the mouse button, and drag the box.

10. (Optional) To change the order in which the areas are recognized, click on the Order Zones button (the button with the # sign on it), and then click on the selected areas in the order in which you want them recognized.

11. Open the Recognize menu, and choose Selected Areas. A dialog box appears, displaying the OCR progress.

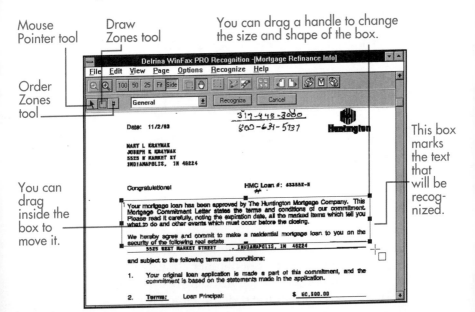

Mouse Pointer tool

Draw Zones tool

You can drag a handle to change the size and shape of the box.

Order Zones tool

You can drag inside the box to move it.

This box marks the text that will be recognized.

Figure 21.2 Mark the areas whose text you want to recognize.

If you chose to save the text in a file or place it on the Windows Clipboard, the text is placed where you specified. If you chose Interactive Text Edit, the text appears in a separate window at the bottom of the screen. Edit the text, as desired, and then open the File menu and select Save to save the text in a file.

In this lesson, you learned how to transform fax pages into editable text. In the next section of this book, you will learn how to manage the faxes you have sent and received and any attachments you may have created.

22

Managing Fax Attachments

In this lesson, you will learn how to group, delete, and rearrange the fax attachments you created to make them more manageable.

In Lessons 6–8, you learned to create and send attachments. As you gain experience with WinFax and generate more and more attachments, you may want to organize and group them for easy access. In the following sections, you will learn to add and delete fax attachments, search for attachments, and create folders for grouping attachments.

Working with the Attachments Window

To manage your fax attachments, you will use the Attachments/Search Criteria Active window shown in Figure 22.1. To display this window, open the Fax menu, and select Attachments. The Attachments window is divided into the following three panes:

Attachment Folders are folders that you can create and use to group related attachments. To view a list of attachments in a folder, double-click on the folder's icon.

Attachments are the individual attachments that are in the currently selected folder.

Information or Thumbnail View is the pane at the bottom. To change what this pane displays (information about or a thumbnail view of the attachment), open the Window menu, and select Display Information or Display Thumbnails.

To change the size of a pane, move the mouse pointer over the line that separates one pane from another. Hold down the mouse button, and drag the line to change the size of the two panes. Release the mouse button when you are done.

Attachment folders

Thumbnail view of selected attachment

Attachments

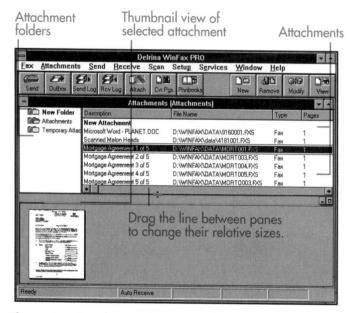

Figure 22.1 The Attachments window has three panes.

Creating an Attachment Folder

To group attachments and make them more manageable, first create a folder in which to place the attachments. Create a folder as follows:

1. Display the Attachments window, as explained earlier.

2. Double-click on the New Folder icon. The New Attachment Folder dialog box appears, as shown in Figure 22.2.

3. In the Folder Name text box, type a name for the new folder.

4. (Optional) To place the new folder inside another folder, click on the Subfolder Of option, and select the folder in which you want to insert the new folder.

5. Click on the OK button. The folder is created and appears in the Folder list.

To make a folder inside another folder, select this option.

Type a folder name here.

Figure 22.2   Type a name for the new folder.

After you start placing attachments in folders, you must have a way to switch between folders to view lists of their attachments. To view a list of a folder's attachments, double-click on its icon.

Folders Inside Folders   Whenever a folder contains other folders, there is a **+** or **-** to the left of its icon. The **+** indicates that the folder contains folders that you cannot see. To see the hidden folders, click on the plus sign (**+**). When the folders are shown, a minus sign (**-**) appears. To hide the folders, click on the minus sign.

Adding and Deleting Attachments

You can add attachments to a folder and remove attachments from it. You can add the following types of attachments to a folder:

- Attachments you created by transforming documents, sent faxes, or received faxes into attachments. (See Lesson 6.)

- Attachments you created by scanning a page and then saving the scan as a file. (See Lesson 7.)

- Any fax you sent or received (whether or not you transformed it into an attachment).

- A binary file (for example, a graphic file or document) that you want to transfer to another computer using the binary transfer transmission method. (See Lesson 9.)

To add an attachment to a folder, perform the following steps:

1. Double-click on the folder where you want the attachment placed.

2. Double-click on New Attachment in the attachments list, or click inside the list and click on the New button. The New Attachment dialog box appears.

3. Click on the Select button, and use the dialog box, as shown in Figure 22.3 to select the file you want to use as an attachment. (If you choose a non-WinFax file, one without an .FX? extension, WinFax will list the file as Binary.)

> **Flying Blind** The file names you see tell you very little. .FXS files are attachments you created. .FXR files are faxes you received. .FXD are faxes you have sent. The rest is guesswork. You can view a thumbnail version of the attachment after it's added to the folder.

4. Click on the OK button. You are returned to the
   New Attachment dialog box. If you chose a file
   without an .FX? extension, WinFax adds a description in the Description text box.

5. Go to the Description text box, and type a description for your attachment. (If a description is already
   entered, you can drag over it and type a new description.)

6. (Optional) Type an entry in the **K**eywords text box,
   which you can use later to help you find the attachment. (For example, type **1994 First Quarter
   Sales**.)

7. Click on OK. The attachment is added to the attachments list.

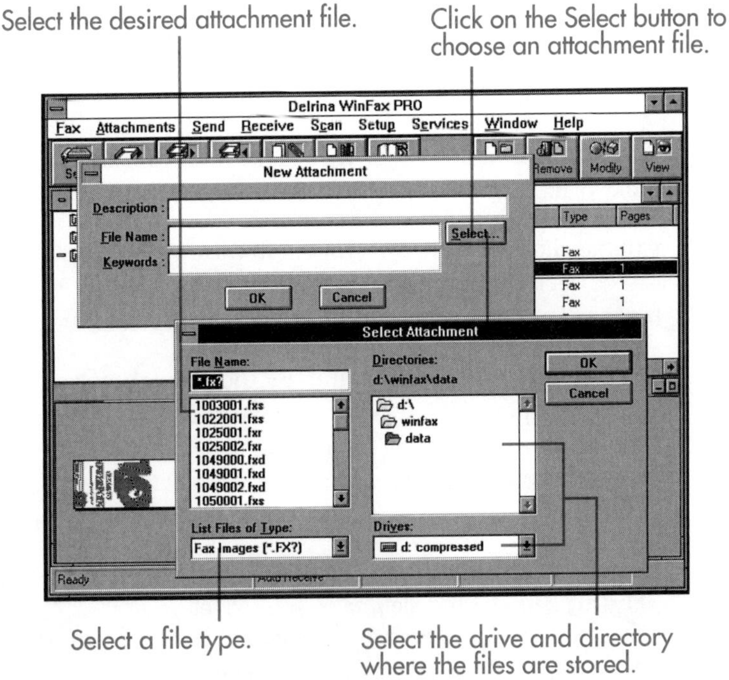

Select the desired attachment file.   Click on the Select button to
                                           choose an attachment file.

Select a file type.   Select the drive and directory
                           where the files are stored.

Figure 22.3   Select the attachment you want to add to the
folder.

To delete an attachment from the list, first click on the attachment, and then click on the Remove button, or open the **Attachments** menu and select Remove.

Copying and Moving Attachments

After you create a folder, you can add attachments to it as explained in the previous section. You can also copy or move attachment files from one folder to another as follows:

1. Display the icon for the folder into which you want to drag the attachments.

2. Double-click on the folder that contains the attachments you want to copy or move to another folder.

3. Hold down the Ctrl key, and click on each attachment you want to copy or move. (You can select several neighboring attachments by holding down the Shift key while clicking on the first and last attachment in the group.)

4. Move the mouse pointer over one of the selected attachments.

5. Hold down the mouse button, and drag the mouse pointer over the folder in which you want to add the attachments, as shown in Figure 22.4. (To copy the attachments, hold down the Ctrl key, too. Otherwise, the attachments will be moved.)

6. Release the mouse button. WinFax copies or moves the attachments to the folder.

The plus sign (+) means the
attachment will be copied.

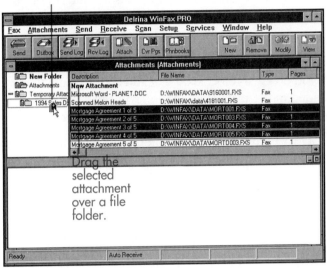

Figure 22.4 Drag the selected attachments over the folder icon.

Searching for Attachments

Finding the right attachment in a long list can be difficult.
You can search for a specific attachment in an attachment
folder as follows:

1. Double-click on the attachment folder that contains
   the attachments you want to search through.

2. Open the Attachments menu, and select Search.
   The Search Attachments dialog box appears.

3. Perform one or more of the following steps to enter
   your search instructions:

   • To search the attachment descriptions, type the text
     you want to search for in the **Description** text box.

   • To search for keywords you assigned to the attach-
     ments, type the keywords in the **Keywords** text
     box.

- To search for an attachment by file name, type the file name in the File Name text box.

> **Weird File Names**   When you create an attachment, WinFax assigns it a number, which you are not likely to remember. You can search more effectively by looking for the attachment by its description.

4. (Optional) To have WinFax distinguish between uppercase and lowercase entries, select Case Sensitive.

> **Case Sensitive Searches**   With Case Sensitive on, if you search for "Account," WinFax will skip over "account" and "ACCOUNT." With Case Sensitive off, if you search for "Account," WinFax will find "Account," "account," and "ACCOUNT."

5. (Optional) To have WinFax locate your search text no matter where it appears in the Keywords or Description entry, select Match Anywhere. With Match Anywhere off, WinFax expects to find the search text at the beginning of the entry.

6. Select Search. You return to the Attachments window which lists only those attachments that match your search instructions.

7. To return to the full list of available attachments, open the Attachments menu, and select Restore.

    In this lesson, you learned how to display and work in the Attachments window, add attachments to and delete attachments from folders, create attachment folders, copy and move attachments from one folder to another, and search for attachments. In the next lesson, you will learn how to work with the fax files you sent and received.

Lesson

Managing Fax Events

In this lesson, you will learn how to manage the faxes that you have sent and received.

What Are Fax Events? Fax events are records of successful or unsuccessful attempts to send or receive a fax. The Send Log displays fax events for sent faxes. The Receive Log displays fax events for received faxes.

Keeping Track of Sent and Received Faxes

Whenever WinFax attempts to send or receive a fax, it records information about the attempt in the Send or Receive Log. You can display the Send or Receive Log as follows:

- To display the Send Log, open the Send menu, and select Log, or click on the Send Log button.

- To display the Receive Log, open the Receive menu, and select Log, or click on the Rcv Log button.

- If the Receive Log is displayed, display the Send Log by double-clicking on its folder icon (see Figure 23.1). If the Send Log is displayed, display the Receive Log by double-clicking on its icon.

Notice that successful events are marked with a green check mark, and unsuccessful events are marked with a red X.

Double-click on an icon to view its list of fax events.   Unsuccessful events   Successful events

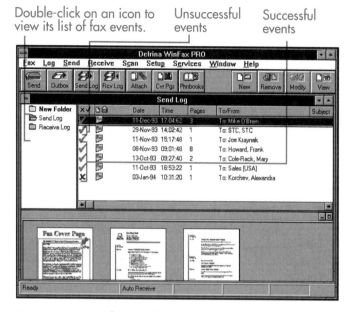

Figure 23.1   The Send Log displays a list of successful and unsuccessful fax transmissions.

Working with the Log Window

Figure 23.1 shows that the Send Log and Receive Log windows are divided into 3 panes. The top left pane displays a list of fax event folders. The pane on the right displays a list of fax events in the selected folder. You can control what the bottom pane displays by opening the Window menu and choosing one of the following options:

Display **Information** shows details about the selected fax event.

Display **Thumbnails** displays a small picture of each fax page that was sent or received.

Display Fax **View** displays the first page of the fax (usually the cover page).

To change the size of a pane, move the mouse pointer over the line that separates two panes. Hold down the mouse button, and drag the line. Release the mouse button when you are done changing pane sizes.

Sorting the Send or Receive Log

WinFax usually lists fax events with the most recent event at the top of the list. However, you can sort (rearrange) the events in the list, to make it easier to find items. You can sort using three sort specifications or *keys*.

> **Sort Keys**   A sort key contains instructions that tell the program how to sort fax events. Each sort key specifies an item by which to sort (for example, Last Name) and a sort order (ascending or descending). Ascending order is from A to Z or 1 to 10. Descending order is from Z to A or 10 to 1.
>
> *Plain English*

Sort your fax event list as follows:

1. Display the Send Log or Receive Log, as explained earlier. The fax events appear on-screen.

2. Open the Log menu, and select Sort. The Sort Log dialog box appears, as shown in Figure 23.2.

3. Click on the drop-down list arrow under **1st Key**, and click on the item you want to use for the sort (for example, Date).

4. Click on the desired sort order: **A**scending or **D**escending.

5. (Optional) To perform a secondary sort, repeat steps 3 and 4 for the **2nd Key** and **3rd Key** sections.

Secondary Sort   Sometimes, when you sort a list, you will end up with multiple matching items. For example, if you receive several faxes from Johnson, and you sort by last name, you will end up with a list of unsorted fax events for Johnson. You can sort these items by entering a **2**nd Key sort for date or some other entry.

6. Click on the Apply button. WinFax returns you to the list, and displays the items in the specified sort order.

Returning the List to Its Original Form   You can return the list to its original form by repeating the steps above and setting the 1st key to Date, the 2nd key to Type, and the 3rd key to To/From in descending order.

Figure 23.2   Use the Sort Log dialog box to sort your fax events.

Deleting Fax Events

The Send and Receive Logs can get cluttered quickly with old records and records of unsuccessful attempts. To remove records you no longer need, you have two options. You can delete the records (including any pages that are associated with the records), or you can archive the records. Archiving keeps the records on disk, but moves them into a separate folder. To delete records from a log, do the following:

1. Display the Log containing the fax events you want to delete.

2. Hold down the Ctrl key while clicking on each event to be deleted. (To select several neighboring events, hold down the Shift key, and click on the first and last events in the group.)

3. Open the Log menu, and select Remove, or click on the Remove button in the button bar. A dialog box appears, asking for your confirmation as shown in Figure 23.3.

4. Click on the Yes button to continue with the deletion, or click on No to cancel the command.

5. Select either, none, or both of the following options:

   Delete Pages (Keep Event) deletcs any fax pages sent, including the cover page. The record of the event will not be deleted; the record is hidden until you redisplay the log.

   Delete Attachment deletes attachment files sent with the fax.

   Choose neither option, and only the record of the fax event is removed from the Log. The fax pages and attachment files are kept on disk.

6. Click on the Yes button. You are returned to the Send or Receive Log, and the records you deleted are removed from the list.

Figure 23.3   You must tell WinFax what to delete and what not to delete.

Archiving Your Fax Events

WinFax provides you with two fax event folders: the Send Log and Receive Log. These folders can quickly become cluttered with old fax records. To organize these records and reduce the amount of disk space used to store them, you can create archive folders. When you move fax events from the Send or Receive Log to the archive folders, WinFax compresses the fax events so they take up less disk space.

To create an archive folder, perform the following steps:

1. Display the Send or Receive Log, as explained earlier.

2. Double-click on the New Folder icon. The New Archive Folder dialog box appears, as shown in Figure 23.4.

3. In the Folder Name text box, type a name for the new folder.

4. Press the Tab key. WinFax inserts a file name in the File Name box. (You can change the file name or location if desired.)

5. (Optional) To make a folder inside another folder, click on the Subfolder Of option, and select the folder in which you want to insert the new folder.

6. Click on the OK button. The folder is created and appears in the Folder list.

Figure 23.4 You can create archive files to store your fax events.

Folders Inside Folders When a folder contains other folders, a + or - appears beside its icon. A + indicates that the folder contains folders that you cannot see. To see these folders, click on the plus sign (+). When the folders are displayed, a minus sign (-) appears. To hide the folders again, click on the minus sign.

You can add, copy or move fax events from one folder to another as follows:

1. Make sure the desired archive folder icon is displayed.

2. Double-click on the folder that contains the events you want to archive. You can archive files from the Send or Receive Log.

3. Hold down the Ctrl key, and click on each event to be archived. (To select several neighboring events, hold down the Shift key as you click on the first and last event in the group.)

4. Move the mouse pointer over one of the selected events.

5. Hold down the mouse button, and drag the mouse pointer over the archive folder in which you want to add the events.

6. Release the mouse button. WinFax displays a dialog box showing the progress of the archiving process. WinFax compresses the fax files and stuffs them into the archive file.

Where Are the Archived Files? You can treat archived files in much the same way as normal send and receive fax events. Double-click on the Archive Folder icon, select an archived event, resubmit the event, or forward it. Because WinFax must decompress the file before using it, these operations may take slightly longer.

In this lesson, you learned how to manage your Send and Receive Logs. This is the final lesson in the book. The following appendixes contain basic instructions on how to get around in Microsoft Windows and how to change your WinFax setup.

Appendix A

Microsoft Windows Primer

Microsoft Windows is an interface program that makes your computer easier to use by enabling you to select menu items and pictures rather than type commands. Before you can take advantage of it, however, you must learn some Windows basics.

Starting Microsoft Windows

To start Windows, do the following:

1. At the DOS prompt, type win.

2. Press Enter.

The Windows title screen appears for a few moments, and then you see a screen like the one in Figure A.1.

> **What If It Didn't Work?** You may have to change to the Windows directory before starting Windows; to do so, type **CD \WINDOWS** and press Enter.

Parts of a Windows Screen

As shown in Figure A.1, the Windows screen contains several unique elements that you won't see in DOS. Here's a brief summary.

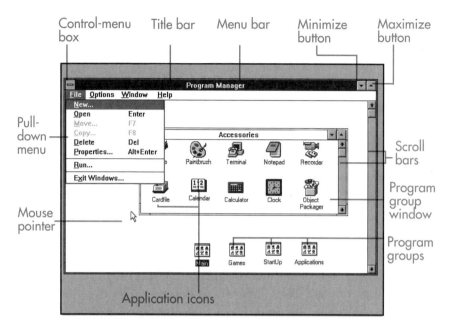

Figure A.1   The Windows Program Manager

- **Title bar** This shows the name of the window or program.

- **Program group windows** These contain *program icons.*

- **Program icons** These are small pictures representing programs. To run a program, select its icon.

- **Minimize and Maximize buttons** These alter a window's size. The Minimize button shrinks the window to the size of an icon. The Maximize button expands the window to fill the screen. When maximized, a window contains a double-arrow *Restore button*, which returns the window to its previous size.

- **Control-menu box**   When selected, this pulls down a menu that offers size and location controls for the window.

- **Pull-down menu bar**   This contains a list of the pull-down menus available in the program.

- **Mouse Pointer**   If you are using a mouse, the mouse pointer (usually an arrow) appears on-screen. It can be controlled by moving the mouse (discussed later in this Appendix).

- **Scroll bars**   If a window contains more information than can be displayed in the window, a scroll bar appears. *Scroll arrows* on each end of the scroll bar allow you to scroll slowly. Click on an arrow to scroll in that direction. The *scroll box* allows faster scrolling. Drag the scroll box in the desired direction.

Using a Mouse

To work most efficiently in Windows, you should use a mouse. You can press mouse buttons and move the mouse in various ways to change the way it acts:

Point means to move the mouse pointer onto the specified item by moving the mouse. The tip of the mouse pointer must be touching the item.

Click on an item means to move the pointer onto a specified item and press the mouse button once. Unless specified otherwise, use the left mouse button.

Double-click on an item means to move the pointer onto the specified item and press and release the mouse button twice quickly.

Drag means to move the mouse pointer onto the specified item, hold down the mouse button, and move the mouse while holding down the button.

Figure A.2 shows how to use the mouse for common Windows tasks, such as running applications and moving and resizing windows.

Right-Clicking in WinFax PRO In WinFax PRO, you can point to an item in a list and click the right mouse button to display a *pop-up* menu. You can then select a command from the pop-up menu rather than opening a pull-down menu.

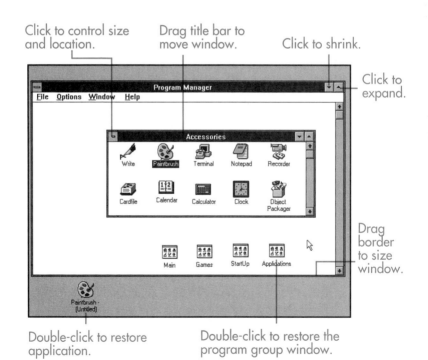

Click to control size and location.

Drag title bar to move window.

Click to shrink.

Click to expand.

Drag border to size window.

Double-click to restore application.

Double-click to restore the program group window.

Figure A.2 Use your mouse to control Windows.

Starting a Program

To start a program, simply select its icon. (If its icon is contained in a program group window that's not open at the moment, open the window first.) Follow these steps:

1. If necessary, open the program group window that contains the program by clicking on the program group icon.

2. Double-click on the icon for the program you want to run.

Using Menus

The pull-down menu bar (see Figure A.3) contains various menus from which you can select commands. Each Windows program you run has a set of pull-down menus as does Windows itself.

To open a menu, click on its name on the menu bar. Once a menu is open, you can select a command from it by clicking on the desired command.

> **Accelerator Keys**   Notice in Figure A.3, that some commands are followed by key names such as **Enter** (for the **O**pen command) or **F8** (for the **C**opy command). These are called *shortcut keys*. You can use these keys to perform the commands without even opening the menu.

Selection letters   Grayed options   Shortcut keys

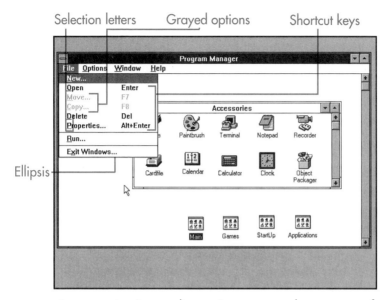

Ellipsis

Figure A.3 A menu lists various commands you can perform.

When you select a command, it is usually performed immediately. However:

- If the command name is gray (rather than black), the command is unavailable at the moment, and you cannot choose it.

- If an arrow follows the command name, selecting it will cause another menu to appear, from which you can select another command.

- If an ellipses (three dots) follows the command name, selecting it will cause a dialog box to appear. You'll learn about dialog boxes in the next section.

Navigating Dialog Boxes

A *dialog box* is Windows' way of requesting additional information. For example, if you open the Setup menu in WinFax PRO and select the Fax/Modem command, you'll see the dialog box shown in Figure A.4.

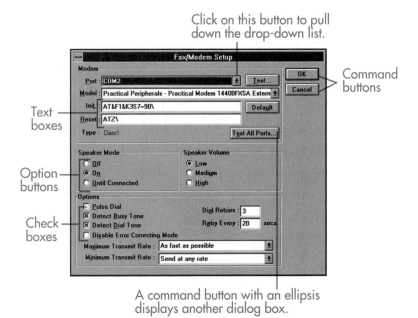

Click on this button to pull down the drop-down list.

Command buttons

Text boxes

Option buttons

Check boxes

A command button with an ellipsis displays another dialog box.

Figure A.4 A typical dialog box.

Each dialog box contains one or more of the following elements:

- **List boxes** display available choices. To activate a list, click inside the list box. If the entire list is not visible, use the scroll bar to view the items in the list. To select an item from the list, click on it.

- **Drop-down lists** are similar to list boxes, but only one item in the list is shown. To see the rest of the items, click on the down arrow to the right of the list box. To select an item from the list, click on it.

- **Text boxes** are for you to type in information. To activate a text box, click inside it. To edit an existing entry, use the arrow keys to move the cursor, press the Del or Backspace keys to delete existing characters, and then type your correction.

- **Check boxes** allow you to select one or more items in a group of options. For example, you can select both **P**ulse Dial and Detect **B**usy Tone. Click on a check box to activate it.

- **Option buttons** are like check boxes, but only one button in a group can be active. Selecting one button *deselects* any other option selected. Click on an option button to activate it.

- **Command buttons** execute (or cancel) the command once you have made your selections in the dialog box. To press a command button, click on it.

Switching Between Windows

Many times, you will have more than one window open at once. Some open windows may be program group windows, while others may be actual programs that are running. To switch among them:

- Pull down the Window menu, and choose the window you want to view

OR

- If a portion of the desired window is visible, click on it.

Controlling a Window

As you saw earlier, you can minimize, maximize, and restore windows on your screen. In addition, you can move them and change their sizes:

- To move a window, drag its title bar to a different location. (Remember, "drag" means to hold down the left mouse button while you move the mouse.)

- To resize a window, position the mouse pointer on the border of the window until you see a double-headed arrow; then drag the window border to the desired size.

Changing Window Panes in WinFax   The WinFax PRO program window normally contains three panes that you can resize. Simply move the mouse pointer over the line that separates one area from another, hold down the mouse button, and drag the line to change the size and dimensions of the pane.

Appendix

Changing the WinFax PRO Setup

In this Appendix, you will learn how to change your modem setup, program setup, user information, and other settings.

The inside front cover of this book contains a quick installation guide that leads you through the process of starting the WinFax Setup program. However, you may run into problems if someone else installed the program for you or if you entered the wrong information during setup. In either case, you need some way to go back to the setup dialog boxes and fix the problem. In this Appendix, you will learn how to do just that.

Changing the Program Setup

When you installed WinFax PRO, the installation program displayed the Program Setup dialog box, which allowed you to specify how you wanted WinFax to perform certain tasks. To redisplay this dialog box and change that information, perform the following steps:

1. Display the WinFax PRO main program window. (See Lesson 1.)

2. Open the Setup menu, and select Program. The Program Setup dialog box appears, as shown in Figure B.1.

See Lesson 17 for details about this section.

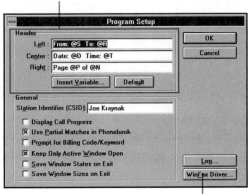

This button displays a dialog box that lets you specify a paper size and fax print quality.

Figure B.1 Use the Program Setup dialog box to tell WinFax how to do its job.

3. Don't worry about the Header section for now. Lesson 17 explains how to change the header (the information that appears at the top of every fax page).

4. In the General area, select one or more of the following options (an **X** next to the option means it is selected):

Station Identifier (CSID)   Type a name, number, code, or company name to give your fax modem a unique identity. This ID prints on the faxes you send and is useful for security purposes.

Use **P**artial Matches in Phonebook   Turn this option on if you want to be able to type a few characters of a person's name and have WinFax find the name(s) that match what you type.

Prompt for Billing Code/Keyword   When this option is on, WinFax displays a dialog box requesting that you enter a billing code and keyword whenever you send a fax.

Show Command Icon Text   Turn this option on to have WinFax show the names of the buttons that appear below the pull-down menu bar. If the option is off, only the icons are displayed.

Keep Only Active Window Open   Turn this option on if you want only the window you are working in to be open.

Save Window States On Exit   The Send Fax log is normally displayed whenever you start WinFax. If you want to open with the window you were using when you last exited WinFax, turn this option on.

Save Window Sizes on Exit   Whenever you start WinFax, it displays the opening window in its default size. If you want the windows to remain the same size as they were when you last used WinFax, select this option.

5. Click on the WinFax Driver button. The WinFax Driver dialog box appears, allowing you to change the fax paper size, print quality, and orientation.

6. Change any of the following options:

Paper Size is initially set at 8.5-by-11-inch paper. To print on some other size, click on the arrow to the right of the displayed paper size, and click on the desired size.

Orientation specifies the print direction on a page. If you send faxes to a fax machine that prints on paper that is longer than it is wide, select Portrait. To print on paper that is wider than it is long, select Landscape.

Default Resolution specifies the quality of print. This is initially set to Fine Resolution (high quality).

To use a lower resolution (and print faster), choose Standard Resolution.

7. Click on the OK button. The WinFax Driver dialog box disappears, and you return to the Program Setup dialog box.

8. Click on the OK button. Your changes are saved, and the Program Setup dialog box disappears.

Changing Your Fax/Modem Setup

WinFax allows you to change three aspects of your modem setup: you can select a different modem, control the modem's speaker volume, and specify how you want the modem to dial. This section explains how to change each setup option.

If you are having trouble connecting to a fax machine or another computer that is running a fax program, chances are the information that WinFax has about your modem is wrong. Perform the following steps to check your modem setup:

1. Display the WinFax PRO main program window. (See Lesson 1.)

2. *If necessary,* disable the Auto Receive feature. To find out if Auto Receive is on, open the Receive menu. If there is a check mark to the left of **Auto-matic Receive**, click on the option to turn it off.

What Happens If Auto Receive Is on?   If Auto Receive is on, WinFax thinks that another program is using the fax modem, and WinFax cannot test that location for you.

3. Open the Setup menu, and select Fax/Modem. The Modem Setup dialog box appears, as shown in Figure B.2.

4. To specify a different port for your modem, select a port from the **P**ort drop-down list. If you have no idea which port to select, click on the Test All Ports button, and then select the port that indicates a modem is installed.

COM Ports   COM is short for communications. A COM port is used to connect a serial device (such as a mouse or modem) to your computer. By selecting a port, you are telling WinFax where the modem is.

5. To select a different modem brand, click on the arrow to the right of the **M**odel option, and select the brand of modem you are using. (Check the documentation that came with your modem.)

6. Do not change the entries in the Ini**t** or **R**eset text boxes unless you know what you are doing. If you change the Init entry by mistake, click on the Default button to reset it.

7. Click on the OK button to save your settings.

Re-enabling Auto Receive   If you disabled Auto Receive earlier, be sure to turn it back on. Open the **R**eceive menu, and select **A**utomatic Receive.

Change this information only if
you have trouble connecting to
a fax device.

Change the speaker volume here.

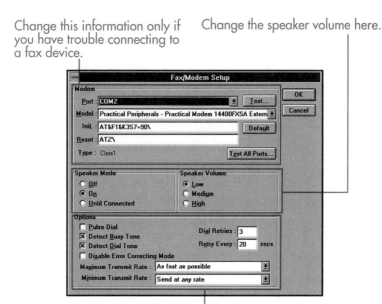

These options tell WinFax how to dial and transmit a fax.

Figure B.2   Use the Modem Setup dialog box to select a modem.

If your modem makes loud, annoying sounds while
receiving or sending faxes, you can turn off the speaker or
change its volume as follows:

1. Display the WinFax PRO main program window.

2. Open the Setup menu, and select Fax/Modem. The
   Modem Setup dialog box appears, as in Figure B.2.

3. Under Speaker Mode, select one of the following:

   Off keeps the speaker off as the modem dials,
   connects, and sends or receives a fax.

   On keeps the speaker on during the entire fax
   process.

   Until Connected keeps the speaker on as your
   modem dials and connects to the remote fax

machine, but then turns the speaker off during fax transmission.

4. Under Speaker Volume, select Low, Medium, or High.

5. Click on the OK button. Your settings are saved, and the dialog box is closed.

The Modem Setup dialog box also lets you tell WinFax how to dial, redial, and send a fax. Enter your dialing preferences as follows:

1. Display the WinFax PRO main program window. (See Lesson 1.)

2. Open the Setup menu, and select Fax/Modem. The Modem Setup dialog box appears, as shown in Figure B.2.

3. Select one or more of the following options (an **X** beside the option indicates it is on):

   Pulse Dial tells WinFax that you have rotary phone service. That is, when you dial your phone, you hear clicks rather than tones of varying frequencies.

   Detect **B**usy Tone tells WinFax to end the call at once if it detects a busy tone from the remote fax. If this option is off, WinFax keeps trying to connect even if it gets a busy signal.

   Detect **D**ial Tone tells WinFax to detect a dial tone from the remote fax machine and immediately end the call.

4. Select maximum and minimum transmission rates from the following lists:

   Maximum Transmit Rate tells WinFax the fastest speed at which to send a fax. (Keep this set to **As**

fast as possible, unless you encounter errors when transmitting a fax. WinFax normally sets the speed to match that of the slower machine.)

Minimum Transmit Rate tells WinFax the slowest speed at which to send a fax.

5. To change the number of times WinFax will try to send a fax before giving up, type the new number in the Dial Retries box.

6. To change the length of time between retries, type the desired number of seconds in the Retry Every ___ secs text box.

7. Click on the OK button. Your changes are saved, and the Modem Setup dialog box is closed.

Modifying Your User Information

If someone installed WinFax PRO for you, or if your name or phone number changes, you can change your user information as follows:

1. Change to the WinFax PRO program window, if necessary.

2. Open the Setup menu, and choose User. The User Setup dialog box appears, as shown in Figure B.3.

3. In the User Information section, type your name, company, fax number, and phone number in the appropriate boxes.

4. Click on the Location option (Away, Home, or Office) that best represents your current location.

5. In the Dial area, enter the following dial-out information:

Dial Prefix   If you work in an office and must dial a number (commonly 9) to get an outside line, type the number here followed by a comma.

Country Code If you (and your computer) travel to a foreign country, enter the country's code here. WinFax will then know to dial a country code when placing calls to your home country.

Area Code Enter your current area code here.

International Access Code If you call numbers in a foreign country, enter the number you need to dial to access international phone service.

Long Distance Access Code If you must dial a number before dialing a long distance number, type the number here.

Off Peak Start Time and Off Peak End Time WinFax allows you to schedule faxes so you can take advantage of lower phone rates. You can enter the hours at which phone rates are lower here.

6. Click on the OK button, or press Enter. You are returned to the WinFax PRO program window.

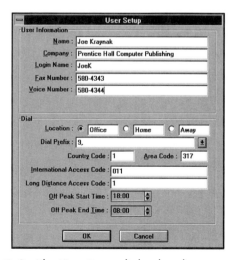

Figure B.3 The User Setup dialog box lets you enter information about yourself.

Index

Symbols

- (minus sign)
    beside folder icons, 124
    in phonebook icons, 86-87
(,) (comma) after numbers in sending
    sequences, 16
+ (plus sign)
    beside folder icons, 124
    in phonebook icons, 86-87
@ codes, 93
    changing in cover pages, 94-96
    changing in headers, 93-94
… (ellipsis), 143

A

Abort button, 72
About command (Help menu), 115
accelerator keys, 142
active window, displaying only, 149
aligning text, 63
annotations
    clip art/pictures, 66-67
    lines, arrows, rectangles, circles, 65
    saving, 69
    text, 62-64
archive folders, creating, 135-136
archiving fax events, 135-137
arrows
    after commands, 143
    annotating, 65
    scroll, 140
ASSOCINCOMPLETE message, 51

attachment folders, 122-124
Attachment Folders pane, 122
attachments
    adding to folders, 125-127
    adding to outgoing faxes, 42-43
    copying/moving between folders,
        127-128
    creating, 31-36
    deleting from folders, 125-127
    finding, 44-45, 128-129
    rearranging within faxes, 45-46
    saving scanned pages as, 40-41
    sending, 16, 46
Attachments command (Fax menu), 122
Attachments pane, 122
Attachments/Search Criteria Active
        window components, 122-123
Automatic Receive command (Receive
        menu), 106
automatic reception, 105-106

B

billing codes, prompting for, 148-149
binary file transfers (BFTs), 22, 47
    sending files as, 49-50
bold text, 63
Border command (Annotate menu), 63, 65
borders
    rectangles and circles, 65
    text boxes, 63
Box tool, 102
Bring to Front command (Edit menu), 68
Broadcast service accounts, 18

buttons, 3
    Abort, 72
    Box tool, 102
    check boxes, 145
    command, 145
    Control-menu box, 6-7, 140
    Cvr Pgs, 94
    displaying names of, 149
    Draw Zones tool, 119
    Fillable text tool, 101
    Graphic tool, 66
    Help window, 6
    Line tool, 102
    Maximize, 3, 139
    Minimize, 7, 139
    option, 145
    Outbox, 54
    Oval tool, 102
    Phnbooks, 78
    Rcv Log, 34, 59, 75, 130
    Regular text tool, 101
    Remove, 55, 82
    Restore, 139
    Send, 15
    Send Log, 34, 58, 74, 130
    Text Editing tool, 63
    Text tool, 62
    View, 75

C

cancelling
    faxes during transmission, 72
    scheduled faxes, 55
case sensitivity
    finding attachments by, 129
    searching for attachments by, 45
centering text, 63
Change Destination command (Outbox
    menu), 56
check boxes, 145
circles
    adding to cover pages, 101-102
    annotating, 65
    borders and shading, 65
cleaning line noise, 112-113
Cleanup Fax command (File menu),
    112-113
clicking, 140
clip art, annotating, 66-67
Collapse Folder command (Phonebooks
    menu), 87
COM (communications) ports, 151

comma (,) in sending sequences, 16
command buttons, 145
commands
    ... (ellipsis), 143
    Annotate menu
        Border, 63, 65
        Shade, 63, 65
        Show, 61
    arrows after, 143
    Attachments menu
        Restore, 129
        Search, 128-129
    Edit menu
        Bring to Front, 68
        Copy, 68
        Cut, 68
        Paste, 68
        Send to Back, 68
    Fax menu
        Attachments, 122
        Cover Pages, 94-96
        Exit, 7
        Outbox, 54
        Phonebooks, 78-80
        View, 95
    File menu
        Cleanup Fax, 112-113
        Exit, 36
        Export, 35-36
        Open, 115
        Print, 9-10, 32, 110-111
        Printer Setup, 9-10
        Revert, 113
        Save, 69, 100
        Save As, 100
    grayed, 143
    Help menu
        About, 115
        Help Index, 4
    Line menu, 63, 65
    Log menu
        Forward, 75-77
        Remove, 134-135
        Resubmit, 75
        Sort, 132-133
    Outbox menu
        Change Destination, 56
        Remove, 55
        Reschedule, 55-56
    Phonebooks menu
        Collapse Folder, 87
        Expand Folder, 87
        New, 86

Remove, 82
Sort by, 88
Receive menu
    Automatic Receive, 106
    Log, 59, 75, 130
    Manual Receive Now, 109
Recognize menu
    Current Page, 118-119
    Select Pages, 118-119
    Selected Areas, 120
    Setup, 115-117
Scan menu
    Scan and File, 40-41
    Scan and Send, 38-40
    selecting, 142-143
Send menu
    Fax, 15-17
    Log, 58, 74-75, 130
Setup menu
    Credit Card, 18
    Fax/Modem, 151-154
    Program, 70-71, 93-94, 147-150
    Receive, 106-109
    User, 92, 154-155
win, 138
Window menu
    Display Fax View, 131
    Display Information, 131
    Display Thumbnails, 58, 131
    Window-name, 146
company names, sorting phonebook
    entries by, 88
Control Panel, Printers icon, 13
Control-menu box, 6-7, 140
Copy command (Edit menu), 68
copying
    attachments between folders, 127-128
    entries between phonebooks, 81-82
    objects, 68
Cover Page Designer, 95-96, 99-104
cover pages
    adding graphics, 101-102
    adding text, 12, 16, 29, 101-102
    creating, 98-101
    editing, 94-96, 98-101
    formatting objects, 102-104
    predesigned, selecting, 27-30
    Quick, sending, 11-12, 16, 26-27
Cover Pages command (Fax menu), 94-96
Cover Your Fax program, 27-30
Credit Card command (Setup menu), 18
Current Page command (Recognize menu),
    118-119

Cut command (Edit menu), 68
.CVP file extension, 100
Cvr Pgs button, 94

D

dates, rescheduling for faxes, 55-56
default
    cover page, changing, 29
    modem setup, changing, 150-154
    phonebooks, changing, 80-81
    printers, setting WinFax as, 13
    user information, changing, 154-155
    WinFax PRO setup, 147-150
deleting
    @ codes, 93, 95
    attachments
        from folders, 125-127
        from outgoing faxes, 42-43
    fax events from Send/Receive Logs,
        133-135
    phonebooks, 82
    scheduled faxes, 55
    successfully transmitted fax pages, 18
Delrina Broadcast service accounts, 18
Delrina WinFax PRO icon, 2, 3
dialing
    default preferences, 153-154
    prefixes, 17
dialog boxes
    Add Group, 84
    Add Phonebook/Group, 78-80, 86
    Attachment Image Creation, 48-49
    Change Destination, 56
    Cleanup Fax, 112-113
    components, 144-145
    Create Attachment, 32-33, 40-41
    Delete Log Records, 134-135
    Delrina WinFax PRO Send, 10-12,
        15-17, 20, 24-25, 27-30, 32,
        42-43, 48-49, 52, 57, 83-86
    Export, 35-36
    Forward, 75-76
    Graphics Attributes, 66-67
    Modem Setup, 151-154
    Modify Recipient - (Default), 49-50
    navigating, 21
    New Archive Folder, 135-136
    New Attachment, 125-126
    New Attachment Folder, 124
    New Cover Page, 99-100
    New Recipient - (Default), 20-24, 49-50
    Print, 9, 10, 32

Print Page(s), 110-111
Printer Setup, 9-10
Program Setup, 70-71, 93-94, 147-150
Programs Available, 49-50
prompting for billing codes and
    keywords, 148-149
Receive Setup, 106-109
Recognition Setup, 115-118
Schedule, 55-56
Schedule/Modify Events, 52-53
Search, 89-90
Search Attachments, 44-45, 128-129
Select Attachment Files, 48
Select Attachments, 43-44, 48
Select Cover Page, 27-29
Send, 76-77, 80, 88-89
Send Options, 17-19, 57
Sort Log, 132-133
Status, 71-72
User Setup, 92, 154-155
WinFax Driver, 149-150
WinFax PRO Status, 12-13, 17
Display Fax View command (Window
    menu), 131
Display Information command (Window
    menu), 131
Display Thumbnails command (Window
    menu), 58, 131
documents, 31
    creating attachments from, 31-33
    scanning, 38-41
double-clicking, 140
dragging, 141
Draw Zones tool, 119
drop-down lists, 145

E

editing
    cover pages, 94-96, 98-101
    headers, 93-94
    phonebook entries, 24
    text in text boxes, 63
ellipsis (…), 143
Exit command
    Fax menu, 7
    File menu, 36
exiting
    Help window, 6
    WinFax PRO, 7
Expand Folder command (Phonebooks
    menu), 87
Export command (File menu), 35-36

extensions
    phone numbers, 22
    files, *see* files, extensions

F

Fax command (Send menu), 15-17
fax events, 130
    archiving, 135-137
    deleting from Send/Receive Logs,
        133-135
    displaying, 130-131
    sorting, 132-133
Fax/Modem command (Setup menu),
    150-154
faxes
    adding/deleting attachments, 42-43
    annotating
        clip art/pictures, 66-67
        lines/arrows/rectangles/circles, 65
        text, 62-64
    cancelling
        during transmission, 72
        scheduled, 55
    creating attachments from, 33-36
    deleting transmitted pages, 18
    forwarding, 75-77
    monitoring transmissions, 70-73
    previewing, 18, 57-58, 75
    rearranging attachments, 45-46
    receiving
        automatic versus manual reception,
            105-106
        cleaning line noise, 112-113
        manually, 109
        setting preferences for, 106-109
        transforming text into editable
            text, 115-121
        viewing/printing, 110-111
    rescheduling, 55-56
    resending, 74-75
    scheduling, 52-54
    sending
        from Windows applications, 8-13
        from WinFax PRO, 14-19
        setting preferences for, 17-19
        to groups, 85
    viewing, 58-60
files
    attaching on-the-fly, 47-49
    extensions
        .CVP, 100
        .FXD, 125

.FXM, 35
.FXR, 125
.FXS, 33, 35, 41, 125
  graphic file formats supported by
    WinFax PRO, 66
.WAV, 108
  names, finding attachments by,
    44-45, 129
  sending as binary file transfers, 49-50
Fillable text tool, 101
finding
  attachments, 44-45, 128-129
  phonebook entries, 89-90
    with partial matches, 148
folders
  archive, creating, 135-136
  attachment, 122-128
  creating, 98
formatting
  cover page objects, 102-104
  text boxes, 63
  text in text boxes, 63-64
formatting ribbon, displaying in Viewer,
  61-62
Forward command (Log menu), 75-77
forwarding faxes, 75-77, 108
.FXD file extension, 125
.FXM file extension, 35
.FXR file extension, 125
.FXS file extension, 33, 35, 41, 125

G

Graphic tool, 66
graphics
  adding to cover pages, 101-102
  annotating
    clip art/pictures, 66-67
    drawn shapes, 65
  copying, 68
  formats supported by WinFax PRO, 66
  moving and resizing, 68-69
  selecting, 67-68
grayed commands, 143
groups
  of attachments, creating, 123-124
  of recipients, creating, 83-88

H–I

hand-held scanners, 38
handles, 69, 120

headers, 91, 93-94
help, 4-6
Help Index command (Help menu), 4
Help window buttons, 6
hiding recipient groups, 86-87
horizontal (landscape) orientation, 149

icons
  Delrina WinFax PRO, 2, 3
  New Folder, 124, 135
  New Phonebook/Group, 78, 79
  Phonebook, 86-87
  Printers, Control Panel, 13
  program, 139
international phone numbers, 22
italic text, 63

J–K

jumps, 5

keyboard shortcuts
  Bring to Front (Ctrl+T), 68
  Exit (Alt+F4), 7
  Help (F1), 4
  Next text box (Tab), 21
  Previous text box (Shift+Tab), 21
  Save (Ctrl+S), 100
  Send to Back (Ctrl+B), 68
keys
  accelerator, 142
  sort, 132
keywords
  dialog box prompt for, 148-149
  finding attachments by, 44, 128

L

landscape (horizontal) orientation, 149
line noise, cleaning, 112-113
line thickness
  graphic shapes, 65
  text boxes, 63
Line tool, 102
lines
  adding to cover pages, 101-102
  annotating, 65
list boxes, 144
Log command
  Receive menu, 59, 75, 130
  Send menu, 58, 74-75, 130
long-distance phone numbers, 22

M

Manual Receive Now command (Receive
    menu), 109
manual reception, 109
    versus automatic reception, 105-106
Maximize button, 3, 139
memory
    determining available amounts, 115
    OCR requirements, 114-115
menu bar, 140
    pull-down, 142
menus, 141-143
messages, ASSOCINCOMPLETE, 51
Minimize button, 7, 139
minus sign (-)
    beside folder icons, 124
    in phonebook icons, 86-87
modems
    default setup, changing, 150-154
    Station Identifiers (CSIDs), 148
mouse operations, 140-141
mouse pointer, 140
moving
    attachments between folders, 127-128
    entries between phonebooks, 81-82
    objects, 68-69
    windows, 146
MS At Work technology, 22

N-O

names
    adding to phonebooks, 20-24, 81-82
    recipients, selecting, 52
    selecting from phonebooks, 24-25
New command (Phonebooks menu), 86
New Folder icon, 124, 135
New Phonebook/Group icon, 78-79

OCR (optical character recognition),
    114-121
on-line help, 4-6
Open command (File menu), 115
opening menus, 142
option buttons, 145
orientation, changing, 149
Outbox button, 54
Outbox command (Fax menu), 54
Outbox list
    deleting faxes from, 55
    viewing, 54
Oval tool, 102

P

panes
    Attachments/Search Criteria Active
        window, 122-123
    resizing, 132, 146
    Send/Receive Logs, 131-132
paper sizes, changing, 149
Paste command (Edit menu), 68
Phnbooks button, 78
phone numbers
    adding to phonebooks, 20-24, 81-82
    extensions, 22
    long-distance, 22
    overseas, 22
    prefixes, 17
Phonebook icons, 86-87
Phonebook window, 78-79
phonebooks
    creating, 78-80
    default, changing, 80-81
    deleting, 82
    entries
        adding, 81-82
        creating, 20-24
        editing, 24
        finding, 89-90
        finding with partial matches, 148
        selecting, 24-25
        sorting, 88
    recipient groups, creating, 83-88
    selecting, 80
Phonebooks command (Fax menu), 78-80
pictures, annotating, 66-67
plus sign (+)
    beside folder icons, 124
    in phonebook icons, 86-87
pointing, 140
points, 64
pop-up menus, 141
portrait (vertical) orientation, 149
ports, changing for modems, 151
prefixes, dialing, 17
previewing faxes, 18, 57-58, 75
Print command (File menu), 9-10, 32,
    110-111
Printer Setup command (File menu), 9-10
printers, setting WinFax as default, 13
Printers icon, Control Panel, 13
printing
    incoming faxes, 108
    received faxes, 110-111

sending faxes by, from Windows
    applications, 8-13
Program command (Setup menu), 70-71,
    93-94, 147-150
program group windows, 139
program icons, 139
programs
    Cover Your Fax, 27-30
    Scanner, 38-41
    starting in Windows, 142
pull-down menu bar, 140, 142

Q-R

Quick Cover Pages, sending, 11-12, 16,
    26-27
quick faxes, sending, 8-19

Rcv Log button, 34, 59, 75, 130
Receive command (Setup menu), 106-109
Receive Log
    deleting fax events, 133-135
    displaying, 130-131
    sorting fax events, 132-133
    window panes, 131-132
Receive Log window, 34
receiving faxes
    cleaning line noise, 112-113
    manually, 109
        versus automatically, 105-106
    setting preferences, 106-109
    transforming text into editable text,
        115-121
    viewing/printing, 110-111
recipient groups
    creating, 83-88
    displaying/hiding, 86-87
    sending faxes to, 85
recipients
    changing, 56
    selecting, 52
rectangles
    adding to cover pages, 101-102
    annotating, 65
    borders and shading, 65
Regular text tool, 101
reject character, 116
relayering objects, 68
Remove button, 55, 82
Remove command
    Log menu, 134-135
    Outbox menu, 55
    Phonebooks menu, 82

Reschedule command (Outbox menu),
    55-56
resending faxes, 74-75
resizing
    objects, 68-69
    window panes, 123, 132, 146
    windows, 146
resolution, 18, 149-150
Restore button, 139
Restore command (Attachments
    menu), 129
Resubmit command (Log menu), 75
Revert command (File menu), 113
right-aligning text, 63
right-clicking, 141

S

Save As command (File menu), 100
Save command (File menu), 69, 100
saving
    annotations, 69
    cleaned faxes, 113
    scanned pages as attachments, 40-41
    window states/sizes upon exiting, 149
Scan and File command (Scan menu),
    40-41
Scan and Send command (Scan menu),
    38-40
Scanner program window, 38-41
scanners, 37-38
scanning documents
    saving as attachments, 40-41
    sending, 38-40
scheduling faxes, 52-54
    cancelling, 55
    rescheduling, 55-56
screens
    Windows components, 138-140
    WinFax PRO, 3-4
scroll bars, 140
Search command (Attachments menu),
    128-129
Select Pages command (Recognize menu),
    118-119
Selected Areas command (Recognize
    menu), 120
Send button, 15
Send Log
    deleting fax events, 133-135
    displaying, 73, 130-131
    sorting fax events, 132-133
    window panes, 131-132

Send Log button, 34, 58, 74, 130
Send to Back command (Edit menu), 68
sending
    attachments, 16, 46
    cover pages, 11-12, 16, 26-27
    faxes
        from Windows applications, 8-13
        from WinFax PRO, 14-19
        monitoring transmissions, 70-72
        setting preferences, 17-19
        to groups, 85
    files as binary file transfers, 49-50
    scanning documents and, 38-40
Setup command (Recognize menu),
    115-117
Shade command (Annotate menu), 63, 65
shading
    rectangles and circles, 65
    text boxes, 63
Show command (Annotate menu), 61
Sort by commands (Phonebooks
    menu), 88
Sort command (Log menu), 132-133
sort keys, 132
sorting
    fax events in Send/Receive Logs,
        132-133
    phonebook entries, 88
sounds
    modems, turning on/off and setting
        volumes, 152-153
    notifying of incoming faxes, 108
stacks, relayering objects, 68
starting
    programs in Windows, 142
    Windows, 138
    WinFax PRO, 1-4
Station Identifiers (CSIDs), 148

T-V

text
    adding to cover pages, 12, 16, 29,
        101-102
    annotating to faxes, 62-64
    editing in text boxes, 63
    formatting in text boxes, 63-64
    in received faxes, transforming into
        editable text, 115-121
text boxes, 145
    formatting, 63
    moving between, 21
Text Editing tool, 63

Text tool, 62
thumbnails, 58
times, rescheduling for faxes, 55-56
title bar, 139
Twain-compatible scanners, 37
type sizes and styles, 64

underlined text, 63
User command (Setup menu), 92, 154-155
user information, changing, 91-92, 154-155

vertical (portrait) orientation, 149
View button, 75
View command (Fax menu), 95
Viewer, 59-62
voice calls, 23

W-Z

.WAV file extension, 108
win command, 138
Window-name commands (Window
    menu), 146
Windows
    applications, sending faxes, 8-13
    screen components, 138-140
    starting, 138
windows
    active, displaying only, 149
    Attachments/Search Criteria Active
        components, 122-123
    Cover Pages, 94-95
    maximizing, 3, 139
    minimizing, 7, 139
    moving, 146
    panes
        resizing, 132, 146
        Send/Receive Logs, 131-132
    Phonebook, 78-79
    program group, 139
    Receive/Send Logs, 34
    resizing, 146
    restoring, 139
    Scanner program, 38-41
    states/sizes, saving upon exiting, 149
    switching between, 145-146
WinFax PRO
    changing default setup, 147-150
    exiting, 7
    opening screen, 3-4
    setting as default printer, 13
    starting, 1-4

zooming cover pages, 100